THE STORY OF CANADA

The STORY of CANADA

E.L. Marsh

Revised & Updated by
Mary Austin Faulkner

SPREADING THE FEAST

The Story of Canada
Copyright © 2021 Mary Austin Faulkner

Published by Spreading the Feast Press, Peterborough, Ontario, Canada
www.spreadingthefeastpress.com

Revised and Updated by Mary Austin Faulkner

Cover image: French Rapids by Paul Kane (1810–1871)

Source in Public Domain: E.L. Marsh, The Story of Canada (London/Edinburgh/New York: Thomas Nelson and Sons Ltd, [n.d]).

Paperback ISBN: 978-1-77484-032-0
Ebook ISBN: 978-1-77484-033-7

Contents

Editor's Preface   v

Part 1: Canada Under French Rule

Chapter 1
Finding the New World   1

  Christopher Columbus

  John Cabot

Chapter 2
The First Explorer in Canada and the People He Found   13

  Jacques Cartier

  The Mound-Builders and the First Nations

Chapter 3
Colonizers and Missionaries   29

  The Father of New France

  Brébeuf and His Helpers

Chapter 4
The Young Colony   45

  The Heroes of the Long Sault (1660)

  Laval and Talon

  La Salle

Chapter 5
Frontenac and His Times   59

  Frontenac

  The Story of Castle Dangerous (1692)

Chapter 6
The French and the English in the New World — 69

The Acadians

Wolfe and Montcalm

The Capture of Quebec (1759)

PART 2 CANADA UNDER BRITISH RULE

Chapter 7
The British in Command — 83

British Rule and Chief Pontiac (1763–1764)

Sir Guy Carleton

Chapter 8
The Loyalists, and a New Province — 95

The United Empire Loyalists

Joseph Brant

Governor Simcoe

Chapter 9
The War of 1812 — 109

Sir Isaac Brock

Tecumseh

Laura Secord

Other Battles and the Close of the War

Chapter 10
A Rebellion and What Became of It — 125

Mackenzie and the Rebellion

Lord Durham

Chapter 11
Responsible Government 133

   Lord Elgin

   Lemuel Allan Wilmot

   Joseph Howe

Chapter 12
Progress of the Country 145

PART 3 RUPERT'S LAND: THE GREAT WEST

Chapter 13
The Land Beyond the Great Lakes 153

   No Man's Land

   Explorers of the West
      Henry Hudson
      Radisson and Groseilliers
      Verendrye
      Samuel Hearne
      Alexander Mackenzie
      Captain Cook
      Vancouver

Chapter 14
The Fur-Traders and the First Colony 173

   The Fur-Traders

   Lord Selkirk and His Colony

Chapter 15
Some Great Men and What They Did 183

   Simon Fraser

   David Thompson

   Sir John Franklin

   Sir George Simpson

   Paul Kane

Chapter 16
The Father of British Columbia   191

   James Douglas

Part 4 Canada Under Confederation

Chapter 17
The Dominion of Canada   201

   How Dominion Day Came

   The Dominion Extended

Chapter 18
The Canadian West   209

   The Governors and the First Nations

   Mounted Policemen

   The Saskatchewan Rebellion (1885)

   The Railway across the Continent

Chapter 19
The Canada of Today   225

   A Long Journey
      A Lumber Camp
      Timber Rafts

Chapter 20
Our Country and Our Flag   241

Editor's Preface

When I set about reprinting this work, it was originally because it is becoming harder to locate a good quality version of the book. There are many of us who desire to educate with a well-written history book in a narrative, "living" style, that provides a broad overview of the entire country's past, at our child's age-appropriate level. Quality books like that can be hard to come by, and *The Story of Canada* by Marsh definitely fits the bill for our family. I love the simple way she narrates many of the key events through Canada's history, bringing to life events and people that seem dry and unrelatable in a textbook, in a way that my young elementary school students could grasp. As I got deeper into the text, however, I became passionate about not only re-printing, but also editing and updating the book. Canadian history, like the rest of the history of colonization, has many sensitive and controversial aspects to it. While I understand the reason for the Eurocentric perspectives or outdated language of those in the past, like the author here, E.L. Marsh, we do not share those perspectives and language today, and indeed are growing in our understanding of the hurt that those perspectives cause. Here in Canada, some of the events and people in this book were making news headlines as I was editing the book. Our history still impacts us today and we are still unpacking many of those effects as a country.

Many parents find a compromise by making edits to a book while reading out-loud. While this is definitely a viable option, I was looking for something a little more lasting–a copy of the book that contains updated vocabulary that we consider appropriate in the 21st century, without some of the biased commentary that I felt would prove a stumbling block for many families. In doing so, there were often struggles about whether or not something should be edited or left in. I have done my best to preserve the author's voice, and I have definitely left in the text comments or perspectives that I do not agree with or endorse, while removing the more actively offensive statements. It is my belief that by leaving some of these things in, we actually gain a further understanding of the viewpoints of the past that help us learn and grow in our present. I hope that this updated version of the book will be a jumping-off point to edifying conversations at age-appropriate levels for many families out there.

In addition to discussing the differing perspectives of the author and the historical figures with our children, we can help give children a broader view of history by supplementing this book with historical fiction novels, picture books, and quality narrative non-fiction that portray people and incidents in "The Story of Canada" with more nuance and from different perspectives.

A few examples of updates I have made:
- Replaced many uses of the word "Indian," "savage," "squaw," "red man," "Eskimo," "white man," and "half-breed" to be updated with modern language such as "First Nations", "Indigenous people," or individual tribe names where possible; "woman," "Inuit," "European," and "Métis."
- Edited repetitive stories and words that emphasize the "cruelty" of the First Nations, because when not balanced with stories of the cruelty of the Europeans, it produces an uneven narrative. Some of this may still remain, and I think pointing this out to children would be appropriate.
- Edited overly negative commentary about the First Nations' work ethic, morality, or hygiene. Some of this may still remain.
- Edited over-enthusiastic defense of the colonists' spotless behavior. Some of this may still remain.
- Changed some names of historical figures to the names they are commonly referred to today.
- Added full names for many historical figures, bolded the names of those most prominent in the narrative, and added their birth and death dates for context.
- Added some extra dates for historical context.

Preface

- Added pictures and maps that provide further context and interest for our young readers.
- Updated a few pieces of historical information that have changed since the book was first written–the adding of extra provinces and territories to the country, the adoption of a new flag, etc.

It is my hope that this updated edition will be a helpful introduction to Canadian history for many families, and that we will all work hard to educate our children so that they can write an even better story of Canada in their own time.

Mary Austin Faulkner
Peterborough, Ontario

Part 1:
Canada Under French Rule

Christopher Columbus arrives in America

Chapter 1
Finding the New World

Christopher Columbus
Long years ago, no Europeans lived on the continent of America; no Europeans even knew there was such a place. The people of the Old World then had but little time for learning or travel. They were often at war, and during peaceful days their affairs at home needed attention. Less than five hundred years ago all but a few learned men believed the earth to be flat. They had no idea there was a great stretch of land beyond the Atlantic Ocean. In those days a man was put in prison because he said the earth was round and turned on its axis. But he was so sure he was right that, when they put him into his cell, he stamped his foot and said, "She is turning still."

It is true there were men who had sailed across the ocean, but no histories of their voyages had been written, and the stories told about them were treated very much as fairy tales. Mothers told them to their little children as they put them to sleep at night.

During the time that these stories were being talked about a little boy was born in Genoa. To him the legends of distant countries were told. Little **Christopher Columbus** (1451-1506), for that was his name, never forgot the stories, and when he grew older he believed that far across the Atlantic there might be found a rich and beautiful country. He determined to be a sailor, so that he could sail away and explore the unknown waters.

His father was a wool weaver, and he was intended for that trade. But he longed for a life at sea, and when only a boy began to study the art of navigation. Much of his spare time was spent on the beach, talking to the sailors or watching the waves, and wondering what could be beyond that deep, dark water.

One day an old man who had just returned from a long voyage told him that he had been farther out than ever before, and that he had found floating upon the waves the branch of a tree which was unlike any tree he had ever seen. Columbus felt very sure that it had come from land across the water, and said that by sailing still farther one might come to this land. But the old sailor shook his head and would talk no more.

When Columbus became a man he believed that the earth is round, and that, by sailing far enough to the west, India might be reached. His one great desire was to cross the unknown waters and find out whether this would make a shorter route for the trading vessels than that round the Cape of Good Hope on the south coast of Africa, which was their only course at that time. He also wished to see whether there were any strange new lands beyond those unexplored seas.

Columbus could not start out on a voyage of discovery without money to buy ships and fit them out, and in trying to get help he met with many discouragements. The learned men he talked with declared his schemes impossible. They did not believe that the world is round, and they said that fitting out ships for him would be throwing money away.

But at last the beautiful **Queen Isabella** of Spain heard of him. She was greatly interested in his plans, and tried to persuade the king to help him. Now, Columbus asked that, in return for the honors his voyage of discovery would bring their country, he should be made admiral of all the new seas he discovered. It is said that this request reached **King Ferdinand** when he was playing chess. The king paused a moment and said, "For my part, I am inclined to think the world is square, like this chessboard."

The queen replied, "Surely nothing can be lost by granting a title to this brave man."

Just then the king noticed that while he had been thinking of Columbus the game had been going against him, and, annoyed by this, he said to her, "Speak to me no more of this Genoese, or I shall lose a splendid game. Admiral means Prince of the Waves; too noble a title for an adventurer. Your Genoese shall not be admiral."

The queen was greatly disappointed by such a reply, but she looked at the chessboard and saw a move that might save the game for the king. Just in time she held back his hand, and said softly, "Do you not win, my lord?" The king studied the board again. Then he too saw the move and won the game.

While he was still pleased with this success the queen again spoke of Columbus, and asked if he might not have the title he had asked for. "After all," said the king gaily, "little harm can come from appointing him admiral of new seas yet to be discovered." Before he had time to change his mind the queen sent the message to Columbus that his request would be granted.

Queen Isabella helped Columbus in many ways. She pledged even her crown jewels to prepare a fleet for him, and she induced Ferdinand to help him also. Now at last Columbus saw that the dream of his boyhood was to be realized.

Three ships, the *Santa Maria*, the *Pinta*, and the *Nina*, were fitted out, and one hundred and twenty men prepared to go with them. On the third of August 1492, over five hundred years ago, the little company, with Columbus as their leader, bade good-bye to their friends and their country, and started out on that long voyage that was to take them they knew not where.

On and on they sailed. Sometimes they thought they saw land ahead, but soon it would fade away and they knew they had been deceived by a mirage. At times they would come to great masses of floating seaweed, and someone would shout, "Land! land!" But the cry would end in disappointment when beyond the seaweed they saw only the endless waves.

As the days and weeks went by the sailors became frightened. They lost hope of finding land, and feared that they would never see their homes again. They begged Columbus to give up and turn back. But Columbus never lost faith in his dream. All through the long dreary voyage something kept telling him that he was sailing on to find out for his fellow-men the secret that lay beyond the ocean.

He could not get his men to feel as he did. They did not believe that the world is round, and they were afraid that if they went on they would lose control of the ships and be lost in some treacherous current. At last they became frantic. They said they had been sailing for nearly ten weeks across the unknown sea without finding land, and they would go no further. To quiet them Columbus had to promise that if they did not see land within three days he would turn back. He felt very sure he would not have to turn back, for they were beginning to see land birds and bits of floating weed, and one day they took on board the branch of a tree on which there were green leaves and red berries.

All the third night after his promise to the men Columbus stayed on deck watching. How he must have hoped with all his heart that before the three days were gone he would see some sign of land, so that this great undertaking would not be all in vain. His hopes were to be realized. As he stood anxiously gazing out into the darkness ahead he saw a moving light. All that night a careful watch was kept. The next morning a sailor on board the *Pinta* cried, "Land! land!" This time it was no mistake. As they drew near they could plainly see the green trees and hear the singing of

Finding the New World

the birds. All the trials of the voyage were forgotten now, and with joyful hearts they sang a hymn of praise to God.

Columbus put on a scarlet robe and went ashore with his captains. He carried the royal standard with him, and placed it upon the island which he had found to show that it now belonged to Spain.

As they landed, the natives of the island hurried to the beach, talking in a language the Spaniards could not understand. The sudden appearance of these strange people was a great mystery to them. Some thought Columbus and his men had come down from the sky. They crowded about them, looking at them closely and touching them to see if they were real people. Columbus gave them beads and little bells, and other things which he thought would please them. They in return gave him small pieces of gold, and berries which they had gathered.

Columbus named the island San Salvador, which means Holy Saviour. The natives he called "Indians", because he thought he had reached India. And that is the reason why those islands are called West Indies.

The people of Spain were very grateful for what he had done. Upon his return they gave him a glad welcome home, and Queen Isabella and King Ferdinand received him with the greatest honor.

Afterwards, he crossed the ocean again, and discovered other islands and the mainland. But in spite of this the new continent was not named after him. A man whose name was **Amerigo Vespucci** crossed the ocean later, and wrote tales of his voyage and descriptions of the New World. One of these books was written in Latin, and read by the learned men. By doing this he kept his name always before the people, and so it happened that in time the new continent was called America, after Amerigo Vespucci, instead of being named after Columbus, who had made its discovery his life-work.

Columbus did not reach Canada, but the explorers who followed him and discovered our country had his voyage to guide them. It was he who led the way.

John Cabot
Just five years after Columbus crossed the Western Sea and found land, another great explorer crossed the ocean and reached the shores of North America. This explorer was **John Cabot** (1450–1500). Though he sailed from an English port, and was sent out by the King of England, he, like Columbus, had spent his childhood in Genoa.

John Cabot

We know very little about his early life, but it is likely that he watched the sea and talked with the sailors, just as Columbus had done. There is one story about him which has come down to us, but that is of something which happened after he became a man. It tells how once, when he had his home in Venice, he made a visit to Mecca, a holy city of Arabia. One day while he was there some caravans of rich spices came in from far away in the east. John Cabot asked the camel drivers where the spices came from. "They were brought to us by caravans from farther east," they said.

"But where did they come from in the first place?" he asked.

"We do not know," they answered. "The drivers of the caravans said they had come to them by caravans from a country east of theirs, and that they had come to that country by other caravans from still farther east."

Now, Cabot believed that the world is round, and so he began to think that if these spices grew in a country so far to the east one might come to that land by going west. The more he thought about it the more certain he became that if he sailed far enough across the Western Sea he could reach that eastern country, and that it would be a much easier way to go than across the dusty, sunburned deserts.

Though he wished to sail away to find that land he did not start at once. He went to England first, and lived for some time at the seaport of Bristol.

In Bristol at that time there were many who believed in the stories of rich countries across the ocean, stories that had long been treated as fairy tales and told to children when they went to bed. One of these stories which the children liked best was of a rich island far away in the unexplored sea. Some said that on this island was a never-failing spring of running water, and that those who drank from it would never grow old. Others said there was a fountain on the island, and that all who bathed in it would be made young and beautiful, no matter how old and wrinkled they had been. The men, of course, did not believe the stories of streams and fountains that could make the old young again, but they did believe in a land where rich spices were to be found. Even before Columbus made his first voyage, the men of Bristol had sent out vessels to try to find that land. Though their efforts at first were unsuccessful, they were at last to bring about a great discovery.

Fortunately their king, **Henry the Seventh**, was also much interested in voyages of discovery. Had it not been for an accident he might have been the one to fit out ships for Columbus. It seems that when Christopher Columbus was in despair of obtaining help from the King of Spain he sent his brother to England to ask King Henry's aid, and to show him maps and charts to indicate the voyage he wished to make. On the way to England the brother was captured by a band of pirates and made to work for them as a slave. When at last he got away from them he was ill, and everything he had was gone, even the charts he was to show the king. So he waited until he was well again, and able to make a good appearance at the king's court, and had a new map of the world to present. Now the king was much pleased when he told him of his brother Christopher's plans, and promised to help him. But during this time Christopher had met Queen Isabella of Spain, and ships were being fitted out for him, so he no longer needed aid from the King of England.

When King Henry heard that Columbus had found land he was greatly interested. Later, when the men of Bristol wished to send John Cabot out on a voyage of discovery, he granted a charter, which gave to Cabot and his three sons the right, in the name of England, "to seek out, discover, and find whatsoever islands, countries, regions, or provinces of the heathens in whatsoever part of the world they be, which before this time have been unknown to all Christians."

So it happened that one bright day in the year 1497 a little vessel called the *Matthew*, with eighteen sailors aboard, sailed quietly out of Bristol harbor. The man who was in command was the man who years before had watched the caravans of spices come into Mecca. Now, at last, he was setting out to search for a western route to the land of riches.

Finding the New World

Little is known of John Cabot's voyage across the Western Sea; but from the few writings that have come down to us we know that he did not sail in warm winds that carried Columbus to the island of San Salvador. He sailed north over what he called "that still vexed sea." Then turning westward he sailed on, always keeping the Pole star on his right hand, and at last, after days and weeks had passed by, he came upon land. Some say this land was part of Cape Breton, Nova Scotia. Others believe it was somewhere along the coast of Labrador. This they believe because Cabot is known to have said, when speaking of his discovery, "That sea is covered with fishes, which can be taken, not only with the net, but also with a basket in which a stone is put, so that the basket may plunge into the water." And he also said that from that new country the fishermen could get all the fish they could trade. Now, it is on the coast of Labrador that the fish are most plentiful, and so men reason that he must have landed there.

We know for a certainty that he did discover the continent somewhere along the coast of what is now known as Canada. And so, from the deck of that little vessel that sailed so quietly out of Bristol harbor that bright day over four hundred years ago, our country was first seen by the men of the Old World; and John Cabot, who was in command of that vessel, first placed the flag of England on North American soil.

Like Columbus, Cabot believed that he had reached some part of Asia. Little did he guess what his discovery would mean to the world. Little did he dream that he had discovered a continent so broad that it would be three hundred years before men would make their way across it.

Nothing is told of how anxiously he watched for land, or what he and his men did when they landed, or whether the glimpses they had of that northern coast failed to satisfy their dreams of rich, warm countries. As little is known of their landing as of their voyage, but we know they went about on shore. We are told that they saw no human beings, but they saw snares that had been laid to catch animals, and so knew that men lived there, and they supposed that they had been frightened away by the appearance of the vessel.

When Cabot sailed back to Bristol with the news that he had found land, and had left the flag of England waving there, both rich and poor rejoiced. Four days after his return the king received him at his court with every honor. King Henry, too, believed the "new-found land" was part of Asia, and said that by Cabot's voyage England had gained a part of Asia without a stroke of the sword. Noblemen who had never heard of Cabot before now sought to meet him. Merchants, traders, and fishermen were planning future voyages to the land he had found. Cabot was nattered on all sides, and it is little wonder that he began to dress in splendid garments of silk.

In the midst of his honors he did not forget his friends. He invited them to his home, unrolled his maps for them to study, and presented them with large portions of land in this new country.

Though John Cabot's sons are mentioned in the charter granted by the king, we do not know whether they were with him on his first voyage. But the next year, when he set out upon a second voyage with five ships, his son Sebastian accompanied him. Whether John Cabot commanded the return voyage of these ships we do not know, and we know neither how nor when he died. In the records which Sebastian left he said very little about his father. Later, Sebastian Cabot made another voyage of exploration.

Finding the New World

Though John Cabot failed to find the land where grew the spices of the east, he found a coast full of wealth for the fishermen, and a country which was to become a great and wealthy part of the British Empire. His name therefore should be given a high place among the famous discoverers of the past.

Jacques Cartier

Chapter 2
The First Explorer in Canada and the People He Found

Jacques Cartier
At last **Francis the First**, King of France, began to think about the wonderful voyages that had been made. He had heard that Columbus had found new land for Spain, and he had heard that John Cabot had found new land for England. So he made up his mind that France too should share in this strange, new country. **Jacques Cartier** (1491–1557) was the man he sent across the ocean.

Of course, Cartier looked at the maps before he started. By this time men knew that the New World was not Asia. But they believed that it was just a narrow strip of land with a sea beyond, and it was shown in that way on all the maps. Cartier did not know how wrong they were. It was years before anyone knew that.

The king wanted Cartier to search for a water passage through to that farther sea, and in the name of France to take possession of all the land he discovered. Cartier had been a sailor ever since he was a boy, and was very glad to go and do this for his king and country.

In the month of May, in the year 1534, the French ships under his command sailed away from the harbor of St. Malo. The one hundred and twenty men on board waved good-bye to their friends and turned their faces to the unknown west.

After a long, tiresome voyage they reached Newfoundland and sailed northward. Cartier did not think much of that country, for it was cold and barren, so he turned to the south. After a time, he came to a bay where it was so very warm that he called it the Bay of Chaleur, the French word for heat. Finding there a rich country with beautiful flowers, large trees, and great quantities of berries, he landed at what is now called the Peninsula of Gaspe and erected a great cross. On this cross were the words, "Long live the King of France," and the *fleur-de-lis*. The poor natives did not know that by doing this he was claiming their home for his king.

These natives Cartier, too, called "Indians". Today we use the terms "First Nations" or "Indigenous people" to describe these original inhabitants of the land. At first, they were afraid of the French in their big boats, but by-and-by they went up to them in their little bark canoes. They could not speak French, but they made signs that they would like to trade with them. They brought furs, for which Cartier gave them knives, hatchets, and many articles that he knew would be useful to them.

After Cartier had tried in vain to find a water passage through the country he hurried away, for the First Nations told him of the cold winter that soon would come. They trusted him so much that two of them were willing to go home with him. His friends were glad to see him back and to know that he was safe, for crossing the ocean in those days was very different from crossing the ocean now, and very much more difficult and dangerous. The ships were not like the ships we have, and the sailors did not know so well what course to take.

The next spring Cartier came to Canada again. On the festival day of St. Lawrence, he entered the gulf which he named St. Lawrence in honor of the saint. The same name was afterwards given to the river.

He sailed up the St. Lawrence River until quite near Stadacona, a St. Lawrence Iroquoian village beside a great rock. It was built on the spot where now stands our city of Quebec, and the rock is one of our greatest Canadian landmarks, our citadel, the Gibraltar of Canada.

The First Explorer in Canada

The two Indigenous people who had gone to France with Cartier the year before were a great help now, for they could speak French, and so could tell him what the people were saying.

Donnacona (d. 1539), the great chief of the tribe at Stadacona, and some of his people went out in canoes to find whether the visitors, or "pale-faces" as they called them, had come for peace or war. Upon learning that it was a peaceful visit, Donnacona kissed Cartier's hand and put it around his own neck, while the Iroquois waded out into the water shouting and singing. This was their way of giving a hearty welcome.

After this Cartier went up the river to Hochelaga, another St. Lawrence Iroquoian village, at the foot of a beautiful mountain, which he named Mount Royal. From that we get the word Montreal, the name of our city which now stands where then stood the First Nation village of Hochelaga. Here he had another welcome. These people even thought him some divine being, and brought him an invalid chief to heal.

Cartier did not know what to do, but as he wanted to please the First Nations he touched the chief and said a prayer. Then all the sick and lame from the village came to him, and he had to touch them and say more prayers. Later he climbed to the top of the mountain, where he had a grand view of the country. He was greatly delighted with what he saw, for it was October, and the trees were glorious in all the gay colors of autumn.

But though he was having a very pleasant time, it was too late in the season to stay long. After he had given the First Nations presents, and thanked them for the corn and fish they gave him, he went back to Stadacona for the winter.

Cartier and his men made ready for the cold as best they could. But they did not know what Canadian winters are like, and were not prepared for so much frost and snow. The great river was soon frozen over, and the snow lay so deep that it seemed to the French that the earth could never throw off her thick white covering.

As the weeks went slowly by, and it grew no warmer, a terrible disease called scurvy broke out among them. Before they could find anything that would check it, twenty-six of their number died. One day as Cartier was walking near the river, feeling very sad and discouraged, he met a St. Lawrence Iroquoian man who, but a short time before, had been ill. Upon Cartier's asking him how he had been cured, he explained that it was by taking a medicine made from an evergreen tree called Ameda. With hope and joy Cartier hurried back to tell his men. They tried the remedy at once–in fact, they used up nearly a whole tree, and before long all were well again.

At last spring came, the warm winds began to blow, the ice melted away, and the French prepared for their homeward voyage. It was at this time that Cartier did a very wicked thing. He captured Donnacona and four other First Nation chiefs, and took them against their will to France. He did this because he wanted to show them to the people of his country, and to have them tell the king of the wonders of the New World. They never saw their native land again, but died in a strange country and among strange people. This was the way Cartier repaid the First Nations for all the kindness they had shown him during his stay with them.

The next time Cartier came to Canada, another man, **De Roberval** (1495–1560), came with him. They brought out settlers, and were going to start a colony, but they did not succeed. On his last visit Cartier had done a great wrong to the St. Lawrence Iroquoians, and he now learned that that was not the way to treat them if he wished them to be friendly with the people he brought to live in their land. The St. Lawrence Iroquoians had not forgotten the chiefs he had carried away, and now crowded about him asking for them. He admitted that Donnacona was dead, but said the others were living happily in France. This lie they did not believe, and Cartier saw that they would never trust him again. When they were unfriendly it was much harder for him and his colonists, especially in the cold weather.

De Roberval did not get along much better. He was a strict and often cruel governor, and his people took but little interest in the new life; so, by-and-by, they all went back to France. It is said that at this time Roberval had a niece with him, poor Marguerite, who displeased her uncle by falling in love with a man he did not approve of. In anger, he put her ashore on a lonely island near Newfoundland, with only her old nurse for company. Her love, when he saw that she was really to be left, jumped from the ship and swam back to her.

There the three lived, hoping and praying that De Roberval would repent and come back for them. But De Roberval did not repent, and as winter drew near they built a rude hut to live in, and made clothing out of the skins of the wild animals they killed. As time went by both Marguerite's love and her nurse died, and for two years she lived all alone.

One day she saw a ship far away in the distance. Hoping to bring it to her, she built a great fire on the shore. The sailors in the boat saw the fire and steered for the island to find out what could have started it. Here they found Marguerite, and carried her back to France.

The Story of Canada

Artist's model of the Iroquois village of Hochelaga, in modern-day Montreal

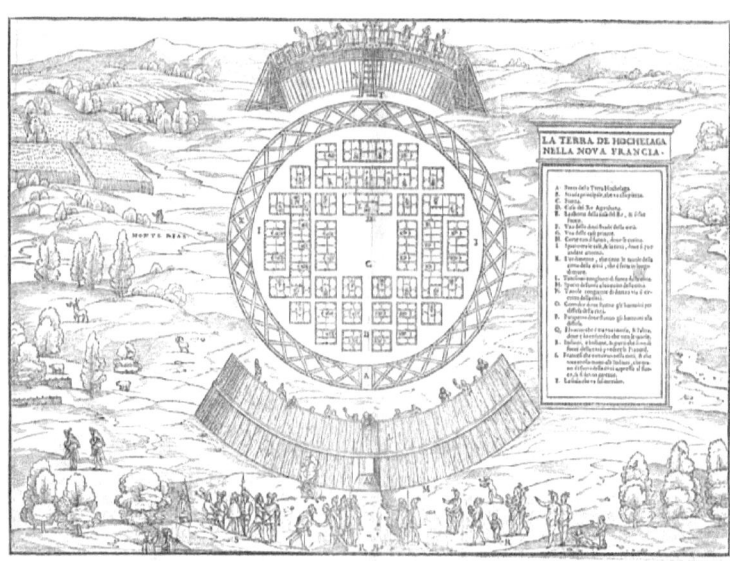

Woodcut engraving of Hochelaga, based on accounts by Jacques Cartier

The Mound-Builders and the First Nations

When the French arrived in Canada there were many First Nations tribes that lived throughout the country. But these were not the first people group who ever lived there. Traces have been found of another people group, called the mound-builders, because they left such great mounds or heaps of earth. In some of the mounds bones of men and beasts were found; in others were tools made with great care, and pottery covered with marks which doubtless had a meaning to those people. They understood mining, for on the south shore of Lake Superior mines were found that had been worked, and from which copper had been taken. In some there were ladders and shovels. All this tells us that they were an intelligent and skillful culture.

We know that the mound-builders lived long, long ago, for when Europeans first found these mines they were filled up, and trees hundreds of years old were growing over them. No one knows where these people came from or where they went to, but it is supposed that what we call the "First Nation" tribes of later times drove them away. Where the First Nations' ancestors came from we do not know either, but many think that they came from the north of Asia, crossing where it so nearly touches America.

If you were to go back to the days of Cartier, you would find Canada very different from the Canada of today. The First Nations' manner of living was not like the Europeans', and the country did not look the same when inhabited by them. They did not settle down in towns or cities, or have large farms, as later Canadians did. They loved the wild forest life, and delighted in roaming about in the woods, and travelling up and down the rivers in the birch-bark canoes that they could make so light and firm. The life they lived made them strong, active, and clear-sighted, and taught them many things that Europeans had never learned.

The Frenchmen who came out to Canada in those early days found the First Nations divided into three great tribes: the Hurons, the Algonquins, and the Iroquois. The Iroquois were often called the Five Nations because they were made up of five distinct nations or tribes. Some years after they were joined by another tribe, and then they became the Six Nations. They are also sometimes called the People of the Longhouse, because their dwelling-places were long and narrow.

Reconstruction of a Huron Longhouse

In those days the Hurons lived in the stretch of country between Lake Huron and the Georgian Bay. The Algonquins extended over a much larger territory. Their homes were along the

The First Explorer in Canada

Atlantic coast, the St. Lawrence and Ottawa Rivers, and westward as far as Lake Superior. The Iroquois had their homes chiefly in the country south of Lake Ontario.

The Algonquins dwelt in wigwams. Though some tilled the soil, they lived mostly by fishing and hunting. They did not always lay up food for the winter, and there were often times when they had nothing to eat.

The Hurons were much more comfortable. Many built houses of bark and poles, and made little clearings in the forest round their villages. There they tilled the soil without the benefit of implements such as we have; but still they raised pumpkins and maize, better known as Indian corn. At harvest time the women would hang the golden ears of corn on poles, which were placed along the tops of the dwellings.

The Iroquois built their longhouses, tilled the soil, and lived very much as the Hurons did.

The First Nation villages were not like any we have seen, for they had no streets, and the houses were scattered about in all directions. This suited the First Nations, who, no doubt, thought their way of living the best; but the French who tried to dwell among them were very uncomfortable, being used to something different. They had no stoves, but in the cold weather built a fire on the floor of the wigwam or hut. Sometimes a number of families would live in the same house; then they would have several fires, usually one for every two families. They had no stove pipes or chimneys, but just a hole in the roof for the smoke to go out; so, of course, when they had a fire, their dwelling-places were apt to be smoky. Though the Indigenous people were used to this, the smoke often injured their eyes, and many of them when old became blind.

The dogs ran about in the houses with the children, and their masters thought so much of them that they would not leave them out in the cold.

In summer they wore very little clothing, but in winter they were warmly dressed in fur. It was the women who prepared the fur for use. Most of the work was done by them. The men were warriors and hunters.

They were cruel to their enemies, but kind to their friends. They were always willing to share their provisions with those round them, and such a thing was unknown as one having enough and to spare and another going hungry. They shared alike in days of plenty and in days of famine, except that in times of great need the last food was kept for the hunters, so that they would have strength to follow the game.

The famine so dreaded by the First Nations came in the winter, when their supply of food had run out and they could get no game. Then they would tie on their snowshoes, take their bows and arrows, and tramp through the forest in search of food.

They liked to have gay times, and were fond of dancing. If a dance was to be given it would be proclaimed through the village, and sometimes through the neighboring villages. They were also very fond of giving feasts. All who were invited must go, for not to do so would give great offence. In some tribes the guests were supposed to carry their dishes and spoons with them, and to say "Ho" to the host when they arrived. Anyone who did not say this was thought very rude.

It is said that some First Nations tribes at war took off the scalps of their victims and hung them at their belts. The one who could bring home the most scalps was a great hero among them.

They believed in many spirits. The Great Spirit who was their God they called Manitou. Their heaven was a happy hunting-ground where there would be plenty of fishing and hunting, and no troublesome enemies. As they believed that all animals had spirits, they looked forward to having their dogs with them in their happy hunting-ground.

Though the wild animals in the forest were so numerous, the First Nations did not hunt them unless they needed food or clothing. When they did go hunting, they would sometimes talk to them and ask them not to be angry with them for taking their lives. The First Nations called all animals their "younger brothers."

Among some tribes there was a legend, telling how in the old days the beasts of the forest could talk with them and always attended the council meetings. Each animal taught the people what he knew. The beaver taught them how to build; the bear and wolf taught them how to follow the trail; the raccoon how to climb the great trees. So in those days, when the people learned some lesson from each wild animal, they gained great knowledge in the craft of the lake and the wood and the plains.

The medicine man was of much importance among the tribe, and they had great faith in his power to cure diseases. He would sometimes do strange things, such as prescribing a feast or a dance, or shouting and rattling a tortoise shell to drive away the spirit that he said was causing the disease. But the real medicine man knew the value of the different herbs that grew in their country, and with the medicines which he made from them he would sometimes perform wonderful cures.

The First Nations had many stories or legends about the origin of the different plants and flowers. One of these tells of the beginning of the tobacco plant. Long years ago, it seems, they did not smoke the peace pipe at their council meetings, as they do now. They did not need to do so then, for they had among them a great peacemaker, a wise old man, who settled all their disputes. When he grew very, very old, and was about to pass away to the happy hunting-ground, he told his people not to mourn for him, for he would return to them in a form that would live forever. After he died the tobacco plant sprang up over his grave. The people smoked it in their pipes, and in the curling smoke that rose from it they saw the form of their old peacemaker. This is why they smoked the peace pipe at all friendly council meetings, and this is why the agreements made when the peace pipe was smoked were held so sacred. No-one would break his word given when the "pipe of peace" was smoked. To do so would grieve the spirit of the great peacemaker who sent them the tobacco.

Among some tribes the sound of the echo was called the message-bearer. They believed that it was the voices of the good spirits repeating their words from one to another, and carrying them higher and higher, until they were far out of the hearing of the beings upon earth, and had reached the home of their God. So they thought that their prayers, if spoken along the shore or among the rocks or the hills, would be carried in this way up to the tent of the Great Spirit.

One of their most beautiful legends tells how, long ago, when a man named Hiawatha lived upon the earth, he first united the tribes of the Five Nations. At his bidding, the keepers of the council fires made the five fires of the Five Nations into one. Then he bade them be friends and brothers and aid each other in all things. At the close of his speech to them he said, "I have spoken, and shall now follow the call of the Great Spirit." Then they heard beautiful music, and as they listened Hiawatha rose in a white canoe and disappeared in the clouds. He was never seen on earth again.

The First Explorer in Canada

They say this happened long, long ago when the world was better, and that as time went by the Five Nations drifted apart, and the one fire lighted at Hiawatha's bidding was allowed to go out. Each tribe lit its separate fire and held its separate council. No longer did they live as brothers.

And so the years went by, until one summer's day, long before the French sailed across the ocean, something happened which caused these tribes to unite again.

Some young people of one tribe had been stolen by another tribe. Much trouble had followed, and war was about to begin. But just at that time an eclipse of the sun took place. "See, see!" they cried, "the Great Spirit hides his smiling face, and will not look upon our battle." And they trembled with fear. Then the oldest and wisest among them rose, and said: "My children, the Great Spirit has drawn his door across his wigwam, and his children will see him no more unless they smoke the pipe of peace which he gave them long ago."

At this the swiftest runner hurried to the village and brought back the lighted peace pipe. The chiefs, who just before had been preparing to go to war with one another, gathered round and hastily passed it from one to another. When the black disc that had darkened the sun had passed off, and the Great Spirit again shone upon the people, the Five Nations were united and the great tribe of the Iroquois was formed.

The Indigenous people at that time did not write. When the different tribes wished to make an agreement, instead of writing it down and signing it, they used wampum belts made of strings of beads. At first they made the beads out of shells, but later the French brought them glass beads. Each wampum belt had a meaning that they understood and remembered. Wampum had other uses too. It took the place of money, and the women ornamented themselves with it when they wished to look their best. One great agreement which was handed down by wampum belts for generations was the union of the tribes which formed the Iroquois nation.

Now all Canada is changed. We have little left to remind us of the past, save some of the pretty Indigenous names that we have for our cities, towns, or rivers. Even Canada, the name we all admire so much, comes from the Indigenous word *Kanata*, which means a group of huts. As we read further we shall learn what part the First Nations have taken in the history of Canada, and how they live today.

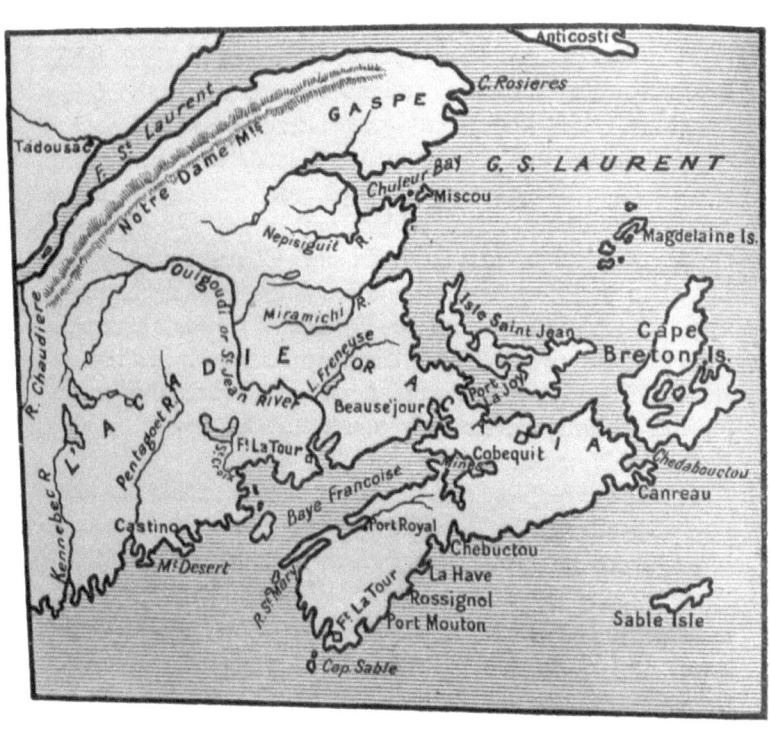

Chapter 3
Colonizers and Missionaries

The Father of New France

After Cartier's last voyage across the ocean the French had many troubles at home, and no time to think about new countries. But about sixty years later they again wanted to start a colony in New France, as Canada was then called, and to have the new country explored. They still believed it was only a narrow strip of land with a sea beyond, across which they might sail to India and China, and they still hoped to find a water passage through the land so that they could reach that western sea by boat. It was about this time that **Samuel de Champlain** (1567–1635) began his work in the new world. Champlain was a brave, wise man, who did so much for our country in its early youth that he was called the Father of New France.

In 1603 two ships were fitted out, and he made his first voyage to Canada. He sailed up the beautiful St. Lawrence River, but the First Nations crowds and villages that Cartier had found were gone. Where Hochelaga and Stadacona had been he could find only a few people wandering about fishing and hunting. After seeing what the country was like he returned home. He took with him the rich furs the people had brought him.

The Fleur-de-lis flag of France from the 14th-17th century

Then the King of France gave a Frenchman named De Monts the monopoly of the fur trade, which meant that no one but he and his men were allowed to trade in furs. In return for the fur trade these men were to start a French settlement or colony in Acadia, which in early days was the name given to Nova Scotia, New Brunswick, and part of the state of Maine.

Champlain was the real leader of this little band, and he was very glad indeed to come again to New France. The little company first settled on St. Croix Island, at the mouth of the St. Croix River. But it was a bleak, dreary spot, and after the first winter, during which they suffered greatly from wind and storm, they set out to search for a more sheltered spot. They decided upon what is now called the Annapolis Basin. There they built their fort, and named the place Port Royal.

During the summer, while the others were busy clearing away the forest and tilling the soil, Champlain went about exploring the surrounding country. Although he knew very little about drawing, he made maps and charts as well as he could. He knew they would be of great use to those who would follow him. But when the cold, stormy days came he and his men were glad to gather round the warm fires in Port Royal.

It was lonely for those few colonists so far from home and friends, but they were determined to make the best of it. To keep them from getting sad and homesick, Champlain started the *Ordre du Bon Temps*, which is the French way of saying the "Order of the Good Time." The order had fifteen members. Each day a Grand Master was appointed, who for that day was to provide for the table. As the hour for their noonday meal struck the Grand Master would enter the dining-hall with a napkin on his shoulder, his staff of office in his hand, and wearing the collar of the order. The others followed, each carrying a dish. Often they invited some of the First Nations to dine with them. Memberton, an old chief, dined with them almost every day. The First Nation women and children, and sometimes the men, would come and sit upon the floor, watching the meal and waiting to be given bread or biscuits, which were a great delicacy to them.

The evening meal was much more simple. When it was over they gathered round the great fireplace, and as they watched the flames and sparks brightening up the gloomy hall they talked of days gone by. Thus, Champlain kept them cheerful and contented.

One pleasant spring morning Memberton saw a sail far away in the distance, and they all hurried down to the beach to see who was coming. A great disappointment awaited Champlain. The vessel brought the message that they were no longer to have the right to the fur trade. Of course, that meant they must all leave Port Royal, for they had no other way of supporting the colony.

Quickly they gathered their things together and said good-bye to the First Nations, who were very sorry to see their friends leave. Old Memberton was specially grieved, and begged them to come again before he died.

Champlain could not content himself in France. He loved the New World so well that he wanted to learn much more about it, and to carry his religion to the First Nations. To his great joy he was soon able to do this. The very next year the king let him have the right to the fur trade, so that he could go back to the new country and start a colony there.

This time Champlain sailed up the St. Lawrence River as far as the spot where Quebec now stands, and it was here that he began to found his colony. What a work he had before him! Many a man would have given up and turned back, but Champlain knew that every beginning must be small. He felt there was a glorious future for the Canada he loved so dearly, and a religion to share with the First Nations. And so he was willing to endure cold, privations, toil, separation from friends, and endless discouragements.

He and his men built a wooden fort to live in, and cleared away the forest round it. Champlain made a vegetable and flower garden, which was a great curiosity to the First Nations. They would stand about and watch him with great interest. As he worked he tried in every way to make friends with them and to learn all he could about them.

The first winter in Quebec was a terrible time for these Frenchmen. They were not used to the cold, and many of them died of scurvy, for they could not find the tree that had cured Cartier's men. To those who survived spring seemed long in coming. How they must have wished for the ice to melt away, and how they must have welcomed the first green grass! As time went by they learned how to make themselves more comfortable during the winter, so that frost and cold had not such terrors for them.

After a time, Champlain's wife came to Canada. Though she stayed only a few years she made a big impression on the First Nation women and children. They liked to look in the tiny looking-glass she wore hanging from her belt. They would go away and say she must truly care for them, because she carried their picture. They all thought her most beautiful, and loved her dearly.

Champlain's great trouble came when he no longer had the whole right to the fur trade, and all sorts of traders came sailing up the St. Lawrence. They got furs from the First Nations for as little as possible, and sold them in their own land, making themselves rich, and leaving very little for poor Champlain and his little colony.

But Champlain would not give up and go home. He would never have been the Father of New France if he had done that. What he did do was to move up to Mount Royal, or Montreal, as it is now, where he could meet the First Nations as they came down the Ottawa River and bargain with them before they reached the other traders. He was always honest with them, and took an interest in them and tried to help them. So they trusted him more than they did the men who sought gain only for themselves, and they preferred to bring their furs to him.

Champlain wanted very much to travel through the country and learn more about it. Besides, he had not given up the hope of finding a passage through which he might sail to India and China. This was the dream of all discoverers in those days. But when he talked of travelling, the Hurons and Algonquins told him of the fierce Iroquois he would be sure to meet. He knew it would be foolish to set out for an unknown country that was overrun with

Iroquois raiding parties. But he felt sure that if he could only get the Hurons and Algonquins to unite with him they could keep the Iroquois in check, and he could travel in safety.

The Hurons and Algonquins thought Champlain's fort very wonderful, and his firearms they called "sticks that thunder." When he told them that he would help them to fight their enemy they were delighted. They promised that they would join together for war, and that after they had fought the Iroquois they would help him to explore the country. Then they feasted, shouted, and danced their war-dances. This was their way of preparing for war. At last they were ready to set out with him to defeat the Iroquois.

It was on a hot July evening that they came in sight of their enemy. Fierce war-cries rang out on both sides. All through the night Champlain could see the Iroquois working so that they might have a barricade of logs put up before the attack was made. In the morning the fight began. Champlain's firearms were new to the Iroquois, and they were so frightened by them that after a few of their warriors had been killed they turned and fled, feeling that it was useless to fight longer with bows and arrows against such strange and terrible weapons as the French used.

Champlain was much pleased with his success. But had he been able to look far into the future that day he would surely have been very sad, for he would have seen that he had made the Iroquois hate the French for coming out and fighting against them. He would have seen, too, that by-and-by, when he was dead and gone, and there was no one to keep the Hurons and Algonquins united, the Iroquois would have their revenge.

After this the First Nations guided Champlain through the country. On one trip he went up the Richelieu River and found the lake now named after him. At another time he travelled far up

Colonizers and Missionaries

the Ottawa River past Lake Nipissing and on to Lake Huron, where he could see the Manitoulin Island which the First Nations believed was haunted by spirits.

For more than a hundred miles he travelled south along the eastern shore of Georgian Bay. The countless little islands were just as beautiful to the Father of New France long ago as they are to us now when we sail among them on a holiday trip.

He crossed over to Lake Simcoe, and journeyed on to Lake Ontario. If you will look at your map, you will see what a long trip this was for the Father of New France, the first European man to travel over so much of our country. No doubt he was glad to have a little rest when the Indigenous people stopped to fish, for they were fast walkers and could easily tire a Frenchman.

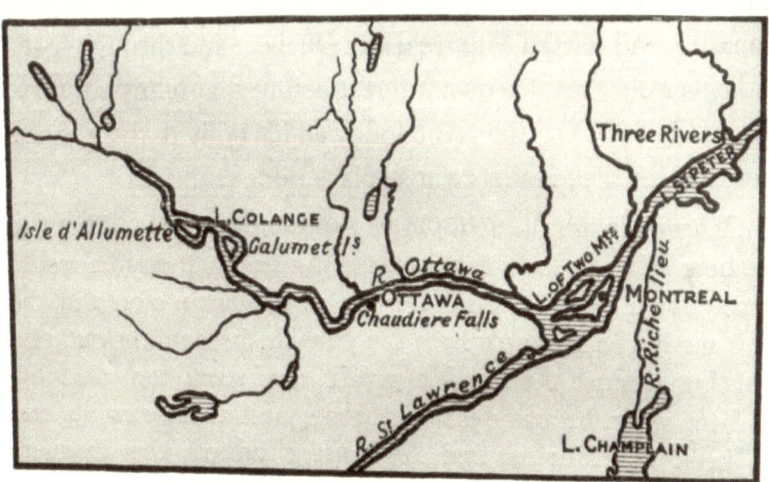

After crossing Lake Ontario in their canoes they had another fight with the Iroquois, but were defeated, for they would disagree among themselves instead of keeping together and fighting in the way Champlain advised. Some of their number were wounded so badly that the others had to stop to make baskets to carry them in.

Champlain, too, was hurt by an arrow, and had to be carried on the back of one of the braves, doubled up in a most uncomfortable position. He was very glad indeed when he was able to walk once more.

When he wanted to go home his guides would not take him. They would not even lend him a canoe to go alone, so he had to spend the winter with them. It was a long, dreary winter for him, but at last spring came, and he was able to get back to the little colony.

After a time, Champlain's health began to fail. Christmas Day, 1635, was a dark day for Canada. On that day he died. He might well be called the Father of New France, for he had given the best of his life to its service. He had explored much of the country, had made valuable discoveries, had helped the first missionaries, and started Montreal and Quebec; and through it all he had never once put his own interest before that of his country. It was a sad band of settlers who followed his body to the grave and mourned for their leader, whose place none could fill.

We now honor his memory by a monument, unveiled in Quebec in 1898.

Colonizers and Missionaries

Champlain's monument in Quebec

A stained-glass window memorializing Father Brebeuf in Midland, Ontario

Brébeuf and His Helpers

Some missionaries came to Canada in Champlain's time to teach the First Nations about God and persuade them to become Christians. These good men made a little altar at Quebec, held service there, and then set to work to become acquainted with the First Nations and to learn their language. In order to do this some of them went to live with them and wandered about with them, paddling all day in canoes, wading rivers or roaming through thick woods, and always helping to carry the canoes and luggage.

When evening drew near everyone would look for a good place to pass the night. Some would get poles and make a wigwam, others would bruise the Indian corn between flat stones and make a kind of porridge.

The mosquitoes were a great source of discomfort. They were troublesome all day, but much worse at night, and far more numerous then than now. The First Nations were used to them, and did not mind them so much, but the French often found it impossible to go to sleep. In spite of all these things they had no wish to give up, but were determined to stay and win the love of the First Nations and bring them into their Church.

One particularly brave missionary who travelled much among the First Nations was **Father Jean de Brébeuf** (1593–1649), a large, strong man well fitted for the life in the New World. One day when he was in Quebec some Hurons from far away on the shores of Georgian Bay came down to trade with the French. Their business over, they wandered into the mission house, looked at the images, and asked questions about them. One wanted to know if the dove over the altar was the bird that made the thunder. Seeing their interest in such things, Father Brébeuf and some others decided to go back with them, dwell among them, and teach them.

It was a long, hard journey, for, of course, it took weeks to go up the Ottawa in the little canoes. Father Brébeuf was separated from his companions and had a lonely time. He pleased the First Nations by taking off his shoes when he got into the canoe, so that he would not make holes in the birch bark with his heels. He always helped to carry the canoes or drag them over the deep rapids. He must have been thankful when night came, even if he did have to sleep on a hard rock bed.

When at last they reached the home of the Hurons they found them very glad to see the "black robes," as they called the missionaries. Brébeuf and his helpers soon had a nice wigwam for a mission house. Here the First Nations were very fond of coming. They liked to watch the clock the missionaries had brought with them, for they had never seen one before. They thought it must be alive, so they called it "Captain," and asked what it ate.

"What does Captain say?" they would ask when they heard it strike.

"When he strikes twelve he says, 'Hang on the kettle,' and when he strikes four he says, 'Get up and go home,'" the missionaries would answer.

So the people, who were anxious to please "Captain," always got up and went home at four o'clock.

At first the First Nations did not care to learn about the religion of the French. They would say, "It is all right for the French, but not for us." Some of them did not want to go to heaven, because the missionaries told them they would not be able to hunt or make war there. One old chief said to them, "If you white people killed your Saviour, make it up to Him yourselves. If He had come among us, we would have treated Him better."

Colonizers and Missionaries

Brébeuf was much disappointed when he found the First Nations unwilling to allow themselves or their children to be baptized. It made him very sad, for he believed that if this were not done they were not ready to die. Sometimes to baptize a child he would drop water on its head, make the sign of the cross, and say a prayer quickly to himself while no one was looking.

By-and-by when the First Nations saw how good the missionaries were, how they tried to help them and gave little presents to their children, and did what they could for any who were ill, they began to think a great deal of them, and many began to follow their religion.

Brébeuf and his friends were so encouraged at this that they hoped soon to convert all the Hurons. They formed several missions among the tribes with a priest working at each.

But their good labor was suddenly stopped in a terrible manner. The Iroquois had never liked the French since Champlain united the Hurons and Algonquins to fight against them. Now that he was gone, and there was no one to keep these tribes together, they determined to have their revenge. So they set out to wage war upon their enemy tribes and the Frenchmen.

The warriors from the settlement at St. Joseph mission met with the enemy on their way to Quebec, where they were going to trade with the French. They had stopped to paint their faces and oil their hair. While they were doing this they were attacked by a band of Iroquois, but as they outnumbered them they succeeded in driving them back.

The little settlement they had left fared much worse. One bright warm morning, when everything was peaceful and quiet there, and down at the mission house Father Daniel had just finished saying Mass, there was a sudden cry, "The Iroquois! the Iroquois!"

Father Daniel ran out, and saw that it was only too true. The enemy were close at hand. Hastily he baptized those who crowded round him and bade them flee for their lives. He himself stood at the church door and was almost instantly killed. Soon the enemy had the village on fire, and those few whose lives were spared were carried away as prisoners. Other villages were attacked in much the same way and burned to the ground.

Poor Father Brébeuf, who at this time was laboring at the St. Louis mission, met with a still more terrible death. He would not try to escape when he heard the Iroquois coming, but stayed to cheer and comfort his little flock. Soon the enemy rushed upon them with their terrible war-cries. They captured Brébeuf and put him to death most cruelly.

Though some of the Hurons escaped to the woods and a few reached Quebec, the powerful tribe was defeated and the mission houses of the good priests were completely destroyed. Throughout the country of the Hurons, the Iroquois were victorious.

Colonizers and Missionaries

A Huron Encampment by Paul Kane

Chapter 4
The Young Colony

The Heroes of the Long Sault (1660)
The land of the Hurons was not the only place where the Iroquois meant to have their revenge. The French down on the St. Lawrence River were in great danger, for the Iroquois were lurking about watching all their movements, and saying they were going to wipe out the French and Algonquins and carry off the good nuns.

The settlers had to be very careful and stay closely within the fort. It was often unsafe for them to cultivate their fields, and much necessary work had to be left undone, for the Iroquois would hide behind trees and try to capture or kill any unwary Frenchman found outside.

With this kind of enemy dogs were a great help. One particularly good dog, named Pilot, hated the Iroquois and could scent them at a great distance, and always warned the Frenchmen by barking furiously. But even with Pilot for sentinel they knew that sometime they would be attacked, and that they were not strong enough to stand against such a foe.

Now it happened that at Ville Marie de Montreal, as the little settlement on Montreal Island was called, there was a brave young Frenchman named **Adam Dollard** (1635-1660) who determined to do something to save his people. Sixteen of his countrymen joined him, and together they begged permission of the governor to go out to meet the Iroquois. The governor consented, and after a sorrowful parting with their friends, who feared they might never see them again, they started out.

They paddled up the Ottawa River until they reached the Long Sault Rapids. At this wild spot they found a deserted fort. It was not strong, and would not be much protection, but it was better than nothing. Here they were joined by forty Hurons, and very glad they were to have their help. All now kept a sharp lookout for the enemy they were soon to fight.

Two or three days after they reached the fort, as they were looking out over the rapids, they saw Iroquois canoes coming towards them. The French fired. The Iroquois hurried away to tell their comrades that some French men were there, and soon they came in crowds to attack the little fort. They found they were not going to make quick work of it, for the French were good marksmen, and shot down those who ventured too near.

The Indigenous people who were with Dollard and his company saw that sooner or later the French would be defeated, and all but four of them went over to the enemy. This made the Iroquois more sure of success. But still for three days and three nights they kept up the attack without accomplishing anything.

During this time the little band within the fort suffered much from fatigue, for they had always to be awake and on the watch, and they were greatly in need of food and water. Being unable to go to the river, they had nothing to drink but a little muddy water found by digging deep down in the earth.

At last the Iroquois cut down trees and made wooden shields to carry in front of them, so that the bullets of the French could not hurt them. In this way they reached the fort. The Frenchmen saw that all was over, but they did not yield. They died fighting for their country and their friends.

These seventeen young men have ever since been called the "Heroes of the Long Sault." They well deserve the name. When the Iroquois saw what a long and hard work it had been for their large number to defeat seventeen Frenchmen they were afraid to attack Montreal, and the little "Ville Marie" was left in peace.

The Young Colony

But all mourned for the "Heroes of the Long Sault," who had given their lives for the colony.

Laval (L) and Talon (R)

Laval and Talon

Two men we must know something about are **Bishop François de Laval** (1623–1708) and **Jean Talon** (1626–1694). They did not fight the Iroquois like Adam Dollard, but they helped to make the colony grow and prosper.

Laval came to Canada in 1659, about twenty-four years after Champlain's death. He was deeply devoted to his Church and his religion, and the Canadians who assembled to greet their new pastor were greatly impressed by him. Their governor said that he was a true man of God.

When Laval came out the fur trade belonged to the Company of One Hundred Associates. This was a body of one hundred men to whom the king had given the sole right to the fur trade and the coast and inland fishing. These men had promised that in return for this they would bring out colonists, help the missionaries, and see after the welfare of Canada.

Laval found them doing nothing but making themselves rich. Whether the colony prospered they cared not at all. Then, too, brandy was being sold to the First Nations, and was doing them much harm because they were not used to the effects of the strong drink. A drunken Indigenous person was dangerous, and one from whom it was wise to run away, especially if he chanced to have a weapon. People sold the First Nations brandy because they would give more furs for "fire-water," as they called it, than for anything else.

Laval tried to have this wrong done away with, and at last succeeded in having a very strict law passed, making death the penalty for selling brandy to an Indigenous person.

After a few men had been shot for doing so a woman was found guilty. Everyone said she must be pardoned. So the governor pardoned her, but he said no one else could ever be shot for breaking the law. After this everyone who wished began selling brandy to trade for furs. Matters were in a very bad way in the new colony.

Laval was in despair when he saw that the First Nations, instead of being converted to Christianity, were being made drunkards. He said a great deal, but it did no good, so he went to France and told the king how matters were in the new colony.

When the king heard Laval's story he began to think about his little colony across the ocean. Upon learning how the One Hundred Associates were behaving, he took the fur trade and all their power in the New World away from them and made Canada a royal province—that is, a province governed under the direction of the king. This new rule in Canada was called Royal Government. It lasted one hundred years. Under Royal Government there were a governor, a bishop, and an intendant at the head of affairs in the colony, and the laws were much like the laws in

The Young Colony

France at that time. The governor managed all military affairs, the bishop had charge of the Church, while it was the intendant's duty to take charge of the money, to see that the laws were made known, to help the colonists, and to look after all the small affairs of the country.

Laval was very glad when he found he was to be bishop under these new arrangements, and lost no time in getting to work. He started a school where young men might study for the priesthood. This school had a department for French and First Nations children, where the boys were taught religion and useful trades, which were a great help to them in after years. Bishop Laval thought that as he was at the head of the Church in Canada he held a higher place than the governor, and he wanted his own way in everything he was doing. Because of this, he had many disagreements with others in authority. The governor, who had called him "a true man of God," found that he was a man with whom it was not always easy to work. But Laval had the welfare of Canada at heart, and he could do great things even if he had some faults.

Talon was the first intendant of New France. He was a delicate-looking man, and some people said he would be of no use in New France, but in this they were mistaken. He was a very great help to the Canadians, as you will see.

He made sure that the people knew what the laws of the country were, for he had them read from the pulpits or put up at the church doors. Then he went on long visiting tours among the settlers to see how they were getting along.

In those days there were two classes of people in Canada: the landowners—seigneurs they were called—and the habitants, or farmers, who rented the small farms into which the seigneurs divided their great lands.

The habitants paid their rent by giving the seigneur part of their grain and by working for him. On each seigneury there was a mill where all grain was ground. It was made very strong, and was a place of safety where all could take refuge in time of danger. Many a habitant of that day knew what it was to hear the Iroquois coming, and to run with all his might from his fields to the seigneur's strong mill, while his wife and children joined him from the little house by the river.

The seigneuries were mostly along the rivers. As the best way of travelling at that time was by water, each habitant wanted a bit of river front on his farm. That is why the seigneurs rented their land in long narrow strips, which were sometimes called ribbons. The habitant had his little whitewashed house near the river bank, and at night, when he had finished working on his farm, he would sit at his door and smoke and chat with his neighbor. The farms being only a few yards wide the houses were near together. These lines of little houses were called *côtes*.

When Talon visited the habitants, he had plenty of good advice to give them. He would show them the best way to farm and tell them when to sell their grain. The children were glad to see him coming, for he made friends with them, and gave much praise to those who were learning to help their mothers and fathers.

He tried to get the people to manufacture things for themselves to make cloth out of the wool from the sheep the king sent out, and to make shoes and hats, and not to depend always upon the goods that came from France. He encouraged them by telling them that when they learned to make articles well, he would send samples of their work to France to show the king what the Canadians could do, and he really did send over barrels of the tar they had made.

The Young Colony

Many of the colonists thought it was easier to wait for what they needed till the ships came in; but one year a ship was lost at sea, and so, until the next year, they had to do without the things it was bringing them. They saw then how wise was Talon's advice, and were more willing to try to make the goods they needed.

Another thing Talon did was to have roads made so that travelling could be done by land. He also sent men out to explore the country, and to search for coal, iron, and lead.

But in spite of all his hard work, there were some English settlements along the Atlantic coast that were growing faster than Canada. The people there were left quite to themselves, and were not taken care of as the Canadians were; so they learned to depend upon themselves, and worked harder than the people of Canada.

Canada had one great drawback. Her young men loved to go to the woods and live with the First Nations. They were called *coureurs de bois.* Of course, in this way they got rid of the duty of clearing the land and keeping the laws Talon had put up at the church doors. When once they became accustomed to the wild life, they were not willing to come back; so they did not help to colonize the country, and were a great disappointment to such men as Laval and Talon, who worked for the welfare of the baby colony.

La Salle

A great explorer, who came to Canada about thirty years after the Father of New France died, was a young Frenchman named **Robert de La Salle** (1643-1687). He tried so hard to find a water passage through the New World, by which he might sail straight on to China, that people in scorn called his seigneury at Montreal "La Chine," because they said it was the only China he would ever see; but La Salle paid no attention to them. He had a great work before him, and no time to listen to such talk.

His plan was to lead New France from cold Canada to the mild south, and to build a fort at the mouth of the Mississippi River, and keep back the English and Spaniards, so that the French would have all the fur trade. He also wanted to explore the western part of the continent and claim it for his king.

He had a hard time, as everyone had who tried to travel about in those days; but the First Nations liked him, and were usually helpful. Any who were not friendly had at least great respect for his friend **Henri de Tonti**. The reason was that Tonti had lost a hand and had a steel one in its place, on which he always wore a glove. If necessary, he could give terrible blows with that hand. They thought he must be a strong fighter if he could strike so hard with one hand, and so did not care to displease him.

La Salle had many enemies who did not want him to succeed, but there was a governor in Canada then who helped him and gave him a fort where Kingston now stands. La Salle was very grateful for this, and promised to rebuild it of stone, thus making a building that would stand for Canadians long after he was dead.

La Salle travelled westwards to the Niagara River, saw the wonderful falls, and at the mouth of the river built a fort to hold his furs. Afterwards he went up above the falls and built a boat—not a little canoe, but a real vessel.

When this vessel was finished he named her the *Griffin*. She was the first vessel to sail on the waters of the Great Lakes; and no wonder they had a great celebration when they towed her out and anchored her ready for her first trip. The French fired their guns and sang songs, and the First Nations waded out in the water and shouted with all their might.

The Young Colony

La Salle did not pay much attention to all this. He was not a man who cared for display, but he felt proud of his work, and he wished with all his heart for the success of his boat. He said he would make his *Griffin* fly above the crows. By the crows he meant his enemies, who were very jealous of him now because he was doing great things.

La Salle and his men sailed the *Griffin* through Lake Erie, Lake St. Clair, and Lake Huron. On Lake Huron a storm came up, and they feared she would go down. They all prayed that the storm might cease, but the old pilot, who was not a very religious man, grumbled, because he thought there would be no honor in drowning in so small a body of water as a lake, and declared that if he were to go down he would prefer to do so in the ocean.

The storm cleared away at last. When La Salle reached port he put on his best robe, which was of scarlet trimmed with gold, went to the mission church, knelt at the altar, heard Mass, and thanked God for keeping them safe on those wild waters.

After this they sailed into Lake Michigan and anchored at Green Bay. There they loaded the *Griffin* with furs, and La Salle sent some men back with her to his fort at Niagara. The men were to unload the furs and bring the boat back to him with supplies.

He watched her sail away, but he watched in vain for her return. He never knew whether the men stole the furs and made away with the boat, whether she went down in a storm and the pilot was drowned in a lake after all, or what misfortune befell his *Griffin*. Her fate remained a mystery.

When at last La Salle knew it would be useless to watch longer in hopes that the *Griffin* might return, he went on with his journey in the canoes. It was autumn now, and the weather was often stormy. Sometimes in landing they had to get out into the water, no matter how cold it was, to keep their canoes from upsetting.

At times they built a rude hut to sleep in, but on many a night they had no shelter at all, and in some parts game was so scarce that they had to go hungry. In addition to these troubles, some of his men, among them two of his best carpenters, deserted him. No wonder La Salle was so disappointed and discouraged that, when in the cold month of January he stopped to build a fort on a hill overlooking the Illinois River, he called it Fort Crèvecoeur, the French word for broken heart. But in spite of disappointments, hardships, and delays he went bravely on with his work.

The longest delay came when La Salle had to leave his men and go all the way back to Fort Frontenac to get the supplies the Griffin was to have brought him. It was a journey of over fifteen hundred miles, and he had to travel all the way by foot or by canoe.

When he returned to his men they went on their way again. After many difficulties they reached the Mississippi and sailed down it not in a vessel, as La Salle had once hoped to do, but in canoes. All this, as you know, was in what is now the United States.

After discovering the mouth of this great river, La Salle went back to Canada, and from there set out for France. In France he got permission from the French king to start a colony at the mouth of the Mississippi River; so the next time he set out for the New World he took some colonists with him. This time he did not go by way of Canada, but sailed into the Gulf of Mexico, hoping to go by water directly to the mouth of the Mississippi.

La Salle had no idea what would happen at the end of that journey. Almost his last act before he left France was to write a farewell letter to his mother, in which he said, "I hope to embrace you a year hence with all the pleasure that the most grateful of children can feel with so good a mother as you have always been."

The Young Colony

But La Salle missed the mouth of the Mississippi and took his people about four hundred miles beyond. There he built a rude fort to shelter them for the time, and then set out by land to find the river.

Disaster followed disaster. One of his vessels had been lost at sea; another, being out of supplies, had had to sail away. The remaining two were wrecked on the reefs. Twice he searched in vain for the Mississippi. Then he tried a third time. This was to be his last journey. It happened that, as they travelled on, food became scarce, and so he sent some of the men who were with him to get some beans and Indian corn, which during his last search for the river he had left hidden away in the ground. The men found this food spoiled, but they succeeded in killing some buffalo. While cutting up the meat they quarreled among themselves, and three were shot by the others. Then, fearing La Salle's displeasure, the murderers plotted to shoot him also.

Meanwhile La Salle was feeling very anxious because they had been absent so long, and finally set out to look for them. When the men saw him coming they hid in the long dry grass, and shot him as he drew near. Thus, in the midst of his work, died one of the great early explorers.

THE STORY OF CANADA

Woodcut of La Salle's ship, "Le Griffon"

Count Frontenac

Chapter 5
Frontenac and His Times

Frontenac

This is the story of the **Count Louis de Buade de Frontenac** (1622–1698), the governor who was a good friend to La Salle. He came to Canada in 1672. He was not a young man then, but he was strong and vigorous and very determined. He was a good governor for Canada, for he knew how to get on with the First Nations, which was a most important thing in those days.

Now Frontenac had heard how the Iroquois had been terrifying the settlers, so one of the first things he did was to send word to them to come out to meet him. They were to meet him at the spot where Kingston now stands. One of Frontenac's reasons for choosing this place was that he wished to build a fort there, where the First Nations could bring their furs.

The governor set out with his men in one hundred and twenty canoes and two flat-bottomed boats, gaily painted in red and blue that they might please the First Nations. They moved rapidly on through rain and shine. They passed in safety the dangerous rapids of the Long Sault, where they sometimes struggled with the fierce currents, and sometimes carried the canoes through the forest and dragged the flat-bottomed boats along the shore. The governor urged on his men while he shared in their labors and hardships. He would not leave his post even when drenched with rain. It was at these rapids that he lost a whole night's sleep through fear lest the water had got into the biscuits. The rapids passed, they glided among the beautiful Thousand Islands, and at last, about the twelfth of July, they drew near to the meeting-place. As they approached, their drums and bugles resounding along the shore, a canoe containing Iroquois chiefs, gay in feathers and wampum, came out to meet and welcome the governor.

Frontenac knew that he must make an impression upon these people if he was to rule them. So early the next morning he had his whole force drawn up under arms, while the drums beat and the bugles sounded, to the wonder and delight of the Iroquois. The governor, in his velvet robe trimmed with gold braid, stood in state, surrounded by his officers, to receive the Iroquois, who gathered about bedecked in the gayest of feathers and paint. He smoked the peace pipe with them, and made a speech in which he began by calling them his children.

"Children," he said, "I am glad to see you here, where I have a fire lighted for you to smoke by, and for me to talk to you. You have done well, my children, to obey the command of your father. Take courage; you will hear his word, which is full of peace and tenderness. For do not think that I have come for war. My mind is full of peace, and she walks by my side. Courage then, children, and be at ease."

After this he gave them presents. He had coats, tobacco, and guns for the men, and prunes, raisins, gay-coloured stockings, and packages of glass beads for the women and children.

This meeting with the Iroquois lasted for several days. During that time the builders were at work on the fort which was to be called Fort Frontenac. It was the fort which the governor afterwards granted La Salle. Before the governor parted with the Iroquois he told them that he was building this fort to be a storehouse to which they could bring their furs and trade them for the goods they needed, and he warned them to trust only good traders "of character like Sieur de La Salle." He tried to make it very clear to them that so long as they obeyed him they should be kindly treated, but that if they attacked the French settlers and their

The Young Colony

First Nation allies, the Hurons and Algonquins, he would send his soldiers against them. The First Nations thought he was a wonderful man. They called him "Onontio." But it was different at Quebec: the people there did not want to be treated thus, and some did not like Frontenac because he would have his own way.

At last the King of France heard many complaints of him, among others that he was doing just as he liked in Canada and making himself rich out of the fur trade. So the king sent out a new governor and a message to Frontenac to go back to France.

There were terrible times in Canada while Frontenac was away. The new governor did not understand the First Nations, and could not get on with them at all. He was soon recalled to France, and another was sent out. This one succeeded no better. Thinking that he would make the Iroquois so frightened that they would not dare to attack the settlements, he sent a missionary out among them to invite them to meet him at Fort Frontenac. When they came, expecting a friendly conference, he seized fifty, among whom were some of their chiefs, to be sent to France to serve as galley slaves. Then he led his soldiers out to burn their houses and their crops and destroy their hidden stores of food.

But the governor soon learned that to deceive the Iroquois was not the way to subdue them. They were not frightened at this; they were terribly angry and prepared for revenge. First they told the missionary to go home that he might not be injured. They knew he had not been told why they were called to the conference. They said to him, "Thy heart had no share in the wrong done to us. But leave us; when our young men chant the song of war they may take counsel only of their fury and harm thee. Go to thine own people." And they gave him guides to take him home.

Then they put on their war-paint and feathers, took their weapons, and stealthily entered the village of Lachine just outside Montreal, where you will remember was La Salle's seigneury. They had chosen a night when a storm was raging. During the terrific thunderclaps and the downpour of rain and hail they crept, unseen and unheard, up to the very houses of the settlers. Scarcely had the people fallen asleep after the storm when they were aroused by a sound more terrible to them than the loudest thunderclap. It was the blood-curdling war-cry of the Iroquois. Children as well as grown-up people, when they heard that sound, knew that the Iroquois were upon them and that their end was near. Houses were burned, men, women, and children were captured and murdered or taken away as prisoners. Such was the "Massacre of Lachine."

The governor, unlike the brave Frontenac, was so frightened that he would not allow the soldiers to march out against them. One young officer, sword in hand, was leading his men on to drive off the enemy when a voice from behind shouted, "Halt." It was a messenger from the governor with orders for them to turn back. The brave officer and his men were disappointed and enraged, but they were obliged to obey.

For weeks the Iroquois hung around Montreal burning houses and scalping their captives or carrying them off as prisoners. Only those who reached the palisades of Montreal were safe, and even there all were wild with terror.

When at last the enemy were leaving they gave ninety shouts to show that they had ninety prisoners. But the French knew that they had taken the lives of many more than that. As their canoes swept past the fort they called out to the governor, "Onontio, you have deceived us, and we have deceived you."

The Young Colony

No wonder the Canadians begged for the return of Frontenac, and great was the joy throughout the colony when they learned that he was on his way back to them. The Iroquois too were glad to see him, for he brought back their chiefs that had been sent away as slaves.

When Frontenac arrived, he found the French afraid, not only of the Iroquois, but also of the growing power of the English in those flourishing colonies on the seacoast which are now part of the United States. They were coming across the Allegheny Mountains, taking part of the fur trade, and growing very friendly with the Iroquois.

The French thought the English should continue to live along the sea-coast and leave the fur trade for them. Frontenac supposed that they were encouraging the Iroquois to attack the French, and he even suspected they might have had something to do with the massacre of Lachine. So he made up his mind that he would strike a blow that would keep them in check.

He gathered together his soldiers, the *coureurs de bois*, and the friendly Hurons and Algonquins, and formed three war parties to march against three English villages. They had a hard time getting over to the English settlements, for they had to walk all the way through the woods and over the rough ground, and the weather was often cold and stormy.

These war parties brought terrible destruction to the English settlers. At the village which was attacked first the inhabitants had been having a party, and, tired after their pleasure, were all sound asleep with so little fear of an enemy that many of their doors were unlocked. With scarcely a moment's warning the French party were upon them. They killed them and burned their homes to the ground. The other two villages were attacked and destroyed in much the same way.

But this cruel deed did not frighten the English, or make them stay behind the mountains. It enraged them. They said that Frontenac had no right to attack them in that way, and that they would not stay where he wished them. They said, besides, that they would never be at peace with the French in Canada until they tore down the *fleur-de-lis* at Quebec and raised the British flag in its place. And they kept their word.

Not long after that Frontenac heard that the English were really on their way to attack Quebec. He at once hastened to defend his stronghold. When the people saw him coming they shouted, "*Vive le Frontenac! Vive le Frontenac!*" as they went to meet him and welcome him, for they always felt safe when protected by their old gray-haired governor.

Frontenac at once had the fortifications made strong, and everything done to protect the town he loved so well. So quickly did he do this that he was ready long before the English were in sight.

At last **Sir William Phipps**, the English leader, sailed up the river with his men and his ships. The first thing he did was to send a message to Frontenac. The French blindfolded the message-bearer and led him up in a roundabout way, so that he would not be able to go back and lead the English up. The message was a demand that Quebec should surrender in the name of the King and Queen of England.

Such a message made the old general very angry. When the messenger asked him to write his reply he made his voice sound like thunder as he shouted, "No, I will answer your general only by the mouths of my cannon."

The English soon gave him a chance to do this, for when the answer was carried back to their leader the fight began. With the great rock before them it was almost impossible to harm the

The Young Colony

French, who from their high position fired down upon them with terrible effect.

October came and the English had accomplished nothing. They were worn out, and their food was almost gone. Then, too, the cold weather was coming, and the river would soon be frozen over. There was nothing to do this time but retreat.

Great was the joy in Quebec when the French saw that their enemy were no longer in the river. They cheered and shouted, and at night, on the high rock, built a great bonfire in honour of their governor. Meanwhile, far out in the gulf a storm came on, and many of the vessels of the unfortunate English were wrecked off the coast of Anticosti, that dangerous spot called the "Seaman's Graveyard," where so many vessels have gone down.

After saving Quebec from the English, Frontenac sent a force against the Iroquois, determined that he would subdue them and stop their attacks upon the French settlements.

In the year 1698 he died. New France deeply mourned the loss of the strong, brave governor who had ruled so well in the days of the terrible Iroquois raids.

The Story of Castle Dangerous (1692)

There were many brave men and women living in the days of Frontenac, and truly there was need of them. Many a story of heroism has come down to us from those troubled times in the long ago of our country. Among them is the story of the little heroine, **Madeleine Verchères** (1678-1747).

Madeleine's father was a seigneur who lived not far from Montreal. As his seigneury was often passed by the Iroquois, and often attacked by them, it was called Castle Dangerous. One October morning, when Seigneur Verchères and his wife were away, Madeleine, who was then only fourteen years old, came out and stood near the river watching for some friends she was expecting. Suddenly she heard a gun. A servant went at once to see what it was, and came running back crying, "Run, mademoiselle, the Iroquois, the Iroquois!"

Brave Madeleine ran to the fort calling, "To arms, to arms!" She at once ordered everyone inside, and set to work to have the fort made strong and in readiness for an attack.

Most of the men were working in the fields. In the fort there were only two soldiers, a servant, an old man, and Madeleine's two little brothers, aged ten and twelve years. All the others were women and children.

Madeleine knew that the only thing to do was to make the Iroquois believe that the fort was well guarded. To do this the help of all was needed; but when she ran through the covered passage to the blockhouse where the powder was kept, she found a soldier so frightened that he was going to set a match to the powder magazine. This, he said, was to save them from being captured by the Iroquois. Madeleine told him that he was a coward. "Let us fight," she said, "for our king and our country."

She then had the only cannon fired, that the men in the fields might be warned of the danger. This frightened the Iroquois, and made them think that the fort was well guarded.

The little company under Madeleine's leadership kept a careful watch, and any venturesome Iroquois who came too near was sure to receive a shot. They were afraid that the Iroquois would come upon them when it grew dark, and all night long they watched. When at regular intervals the Iroquois heard the cry, "All's well!" they thought the fort was full of soldiers, and were afraid to attack it.

Madeleine's little brothers, brave as herself, helped in every way. On the seventh day of the siege, when they were all tired out

The Young Colony

and greatly in need of sleep, and Madeleine was trying to rest with her head on a table, her brothers rushed in with the news that French soldiers were coming to their aid.

It was Lieutenant de La Monnerie and forty men. News of the danger of the little fort had been carried to Montreal by some labourers who had managed to escape from the fields when they heard the cannon fired, and La Monnerie had been sent at once.

Instead of finding the place all in ruins, as he had feared, everything was secure and Madeleine in charge. The Iroquois hurried away when they saw that help had come.

Soon the mother and father returned to their children, of whom they had good cause to be proud.

The relief of Fort Verchères

The Deportation of the Acadians, by Henri Beau (1863–1949)

Chapter 6
The French and the English in the New World

The Acadians

Acadia, the land of Champlain's Order of the Good Time, has many a story. Sometimes it belonged to the French and sometimes to the English. It changed ownership many times while the French were trying to keep the English behind the Allegheny Mountains. Being near the sea, and having no stronghold such as Canada had, it was easily captured by the English. Then perhaps they would agree to give it back, or the French would come and take it from them. The settlers might be living quietly under one flag, when suddenly it would go down, and they would find themselves living under the other.

Matters went on in this way until 1713, more than a hundred years after Champlain took his first settlers there, when France and England made a treaty in which France promised that England should have Acadia.

Almost the first thing the English did was to change the name Port Royal to Annapolis Royal, in honor of Queen Anne, who was ruling in England.

At this time there were some large settlements in Acadia where the people had cleared away the forest. There they had fertile farms on which they raised very fine crops. They had comfortable homes and thriving cattle and sheep wandering over their green fields, making Acadia a picture of happiness and content.

It was indeed a pleasant place to live in, and all might have gone well for the Acadians if they had been content to live under British rule. But they kept hoping the French would get Acadia back again, and some of them even joined the French, who were fighting against the English. The English governor told them that while they lived under the flag of England they must be loyal to England and obey the laws; but they would not change their ways. By-and-by when the English were building Halifax, the Acadians became very troublesome to the English settlers who came to live there.

As the warlike feeling between the French and the English in Canada deepened, the English governor saw that it was not safe to allow the Acadians to stay where they were if they continued to help the French. At last he told them that if they would not live as loyal subjects and obey British rule, they should be driven away from Acadia. As they would not agree, the time came when the threat was carried out.

The story which we have now come to tells of the "Expulsion of the Acadians." It is the subject of Longfellow's beautiful poem, "Evangeline," and is the saddest of all Acadian tales.

It happened that one day in 1755 the people of Grand Pré, beside Minas Basin, were surprised to see British ships sail in and anchor in their harbor. But they never dreamed they were really to be sent from their homes. Not even when all the men were told to meet at the church on the following Friday, would they believe that they were going to be expelled from Acadia. When this message reached them they were just getting their crops in, and they hurried so as to finish in time to go to hear the news the great ships had brought. The little chapel was crowded that Friday afternoon, for the men were all there. Wondering, expectant faces were turned to **Colonel John Winslow** (1703–1774) when he rose to speak to them. Slowly, and in a clear, distinct voice he said, "All French inhabitants of these districts are to be removed, and through his Majesty's goodness I am directed to allow you the liberty of carrying with you your money and as many of your

The French and the English

household goods as you can take without overloading the vessels you go in."

These were the King's orders, and the men now learned that until the vessels were ready they were prisoners in the little chapel, and that they were really going to be driven from the Acadia they had grown to love so well.

Sadly they begged Colonel Winslow to let them go home to tell their families about it. Each day he allowed as many as twenty to visit their homes. The millers went back to work their mills that no one should go hungry whilst waiting for the vessels that were to bear them away.

It was October before the ships arrived. The work of loading them began at once. Colonel Winslow was very good to the Acadians, and saw that his soldiers treated them kindly and were careful of their goods. He always tried to arrange that those of one family should go on the same ship.

It was a sad sight to see these people taking to the beach cartloads of the goods they valued most, trying to keep near their friends, and looking back for the last time at their farms, their houses, and their cattle, before they turned their faces to a strange land. It was still sadder to see the little children, hugging in tiny arms some treasure they could not bear to leave behind.

Much in the same way the people were taken from other parts of Acadia. Altogether about six thousand were sent from their homes. A large number of these formed a settlement in the south, but some after weary months of travelling found their way back to their beloved Acadia, and at last lived as loyal subjects of Britain.

Wolfe (L) and Montcalm (R)

Wolfe and Montcalm

The unfriendly feeling between the French and the English in Canada lasted many years. As the English colonies continued to grow, their interests clashed more than ever with those of New France. The English kept trying to push their way inland, and the French kept trying to keep them back.

Many a battle was fought along the edge of the colonies, a border warfare, as it was called. It was little wonder that the English declared they would put a stop to the French destroying their homes.

One English general, hoping to defeat the French, took his soldiers over to attack one of their forts. He had his men cut a road through the forest as they went along. He was defeated, and his road made a good path for the French to go back to attack the English. Battle after battle was fought, and on both sides fresh preparations were made for war.

The French and the English

After a time, France sent **General Louis-Joseph de Montcalm** (1712-1759) to Canada to take charge of the troops. Montcalm was a clever, well-educated man, a brave soldier, and a great gentleman. He was not a big man, but was active and quick in his movements and of pleasing appearance.

He found in Canada much that did not suit him. The ways of the First Nations were new to him. Their speeches, councils, and wampum belts he found tiresome. But more annoying to Montcalm were the actions of the governor and the intendant. The governor was jealous of him, did not want him in Canada, and would not help him as he might have done. The intendant, who had charge of the money of the country, was using it for himself. He was living in great state, giving dinners, parties, and balls, and letting the poor soldiers go without proper food or clothing. Indeed, he cared more for his own pleasure than he cared whether his country was lost or saved.

Montcalm had to make the best of all these things. He succeeded so well that the English soon saw that they must have as good a general if they were to hold their own with the French. So **General James Wolfe** (1727-1759) was sent out from England.

Wolfe was a younger man than Montcalm, but he had been in the British army since he was a boy, and was now a general, whom his soldiers could love and trust. He was not handsome, nor did he look like a distinguished soldier.

His chest was narrow, his nose slightly tilted upwards, and his forehead slanted back. His hair, which according to the fashion he wore tied in a queue behind, was red, and his face was freckled. But his blue eyes were always bright and clear and his expression kindly.

One of the first things he did was to lead the English against Louisburg, a French stronghold in Cape Breton Island. He guided them up the steep rocky bank, facing the guns of the enemy with only a cane in his hand. Though it was weeks before he could make the French surrender, he was victorious in the end. But he did not have Montcalm to oppose him there. Everyone felt sure that if these two great generals should meet in battle it would be a fight that would decide Canada's fate.

They did meet at the rock-bound citadel of Quebec, for Montcalm hurried there when he saw what a great general he had to contend against. He meant to spend all his strength in holding the key to Canada. Wolfe followed him, determined to drive him out, open the gateway of Canada, and place the British flag where the *fleur-de-lis* now waved. Of this battle you will read in the next story.

A 1797 engraving based on a sketch made by General Wolfe's aide-de-camp during the siege of Quebec

The French and the English

The Capture of Quebec
We now come to the great struggle where Wolfe and Montcalm met face to face at the rock-bound citadel. The French general had seen that all preparations were made. The steep river bank was examined and guarded at every spot where a man could climb. Cannons were mounted on the walls, and soldiers were stationed below Quebec. Soldiers, Canadian and First Nation, collected at the fortress, and all gates were closed and barricaded except the palace gate, which they needed for their own use. The governor boasted of what he would do to keep the English out. The intendant feasted and made merry while he robbed the poor. And so they waited until one June day in 1759 when Wolfe's fleet appeared in the river.

The English general anchored his ships, landed on an island, looked over at the strong fortress, and wondered how to begin the work of taking it. Meanwhile the French governor tried to destroy his fleet with fire. He had ships filled with tar, pitch, fireworks, and loaded guns, and one dark night these ships were floated down the river in charge of a few men, who were to set them on fire and then make their escape.

The English watched the dark objects coming slowly towards them and one after another bursting into flame. For miles around, they made the country as light as day.

The roar was terrible, and bullets flew from them thick and fast. But, though they made such a bright light that moonless, starless night, they did not harm the English fleet. The men had set them on fire too soon. Some floated ashore before they reached the enemy; to the others the English sailors went in small boats, threw out grappling irons, and towed them to the land. From the high steeple of the Quebec church the French governor watched this failure of his scheme. He tried it once more, but the brave English sailors again went out with their grappling irons and towed the burning ships away from the fleet.

Time passed on and Wolfe accomplished nothing. His firing at Quebec could do but little harm, and he had no chance to meet the French in open battle, for Montcalm kept his soldiers behind their entrenchments. Wolfe made an attack below Quebec, but was driven down the steep bank with heavy loss. After that he was very ill for a time, and had to stay in bed in a farmhouse.

Meanwhile the French were jubilant. They felt almost safe now, for it was getting late in the season, and they were expecting every day to see the English take up their anchors and leave. But Montcalm believed that General Wolfe would not give up without making a still greater attempt to take Quebec.

Wolfe felt no fear for his army if he could only get at Quebec, but that was the difficulty. One day when he was better again, as he was looking through his glass over at the rocky bank, he saw a path of which one of his men had been telling him. Above it were the tents of the sentries. This path in that great perpendicular bank of rock was only a rough and narrow one which had been made by a streamlet, now dry. It was called the Anse de Foulon. Ever since the capture of Quebec it has been called Wolfe's Cove.

The general now made his daring plans. He would send a few volunteers up this path to overcome the guard and hold the spot until the army could ascend. This decision was made known only to a few trusted men, but all knew that something great was about to be done. Twenty-four volunteers were asked for. Though they knew not what their work would be, they came forward gladly. Wolfe waited for a dark night. Meanwhile he had the ships with the main part of his army moved above the city.

The night of Wednesday, September 12, was dark and starless. It was the night of Wolfe's choice. At two o'clock in the

The French and the English

morning two lanterns were placed in the maintop of Wolfe's vessel. This was the signal for the start. The boat containing the twenty-four volunteers went first and others followed. Wolfe was in one of the foremost boats.

As they floated silently down the river in the darkness he repeated a well-known poem at the time, Gray's Elegy. He paused at the line, "The paths of glory lead but to the grave." When he had finished he said, "Gentlemen, I would rather be the author of that poem than take Quebec." After that there was silence in the little boat.

The English were fortunate in having learned from a deserter that the French were expecting a provision boat from Montreal that night. They knew that if they could be taken for it by the sentinels they would pass without difficulty. As they floated quietly down in the darkness, a French sentinel called out, "*Qui vive?*"

It was well for the English that they had on board a Scottish Highlander who spoke French with an excellent accent. He answered, "*La France.*"

"*A quel regiment?*" was the next question.

"*De la Reine*," said the Highlander, and they passed on.

To another sentinel farther down who ran to the water's edge to question them he said in French, "Provision boats. Don't make a noise, the English will hear us."

Once more they passed in safety, and soon they reached the Anse de Foulon. Silently they landed. The twenty-four volunteers at once began to climb the dangerous steep, holding on to the bushes when they lost their footing. Very anxious they must have felt as they struggled up the bank in the darkness, for they knew not what trouble awaited them at the top. Had they known more they might have been lighter-hearted. The guard was commanded by Captain De Vigor, a man who had once been tried for cowardice and who was now sleeping peacefully in his bed. He had thought watchfulness unnecessary at the brink of so steep a precipice. So it happened that the volunteers surprised and easily overpowered the sentries.

When the sound of musket shots and triumphant shouts reached the ears of the waiting army they knew that all was safe, and scrambled up, dragging with them several cannon. Wolfe drew up his troops on a rough plateau, called the Plains of Abraham, because a pilot, Abraham Martin, had owned a piece of land there years before. As day dawned they all felt that it was the last sunrise on an undecided fate. They were staking all now: it must be either victory or failure.

Meanwhile, Montcalm had passed a restless night. He felt that the final attack was about to be made, but he knew not where. At daybreak he rode out to look about, and was amazed to see the red coats of the British soldiers on the Plains of Abraham. Bravely he led his men against them, riding on his black horse, waving his sword, and urging his men to fight for the honor of France.

Wolfe went about speaking words of encouragement to his soldiers. About ten o'clock he saw that the time had come. The French advanced, firing on their foe. The English waited motionless, except that as one soldier fell another moved up to his place. At last the command was given to "fire." It was not long before the French lines began to waver. The command was then given to the red-coats to "charge." As they did so they raised a loud British cheer, and the enemy turned in flight towards Quebec.

Wolfe had been wounded three times. The third shot was fatal. As he lay upon the ground he heard someone say, "They run; see how they run."

"Who run?" he asked.

"The enemy, sir," replied the officer who supported him.

The French and the English

Though Wolfe was dying he thought not of himself, but said, "Go one of you to Colonel Burton and tell him to march Webb's regiment down to the Charles River to cut off their retreat from the bridge." Then he added, "Now God be praised, I die in peace." A few moments after he died.

Montcalm, too, was fatally wounded. Two soldiers seeing him hastened to his side, and supported him as he rode through the gate. "It is nothing. Do not be grieved on my account, good friends," he said to those who gathered about him.

He was carried to the house of a surgeon, and when told that he could not live, replied, "So much the better. I shall not live to see the surrender of Quebec."

At four o'clock the next morning he died. Quebec was all in confusion, and there was no one to make him a fitting coffin. A few rough boards were put together, and in that he was placed. That very evening his body was carried to the Ursuline convent and buried in a cavity made by the bursting of an English shell. There were devoted officers, soldiers, and women and children too, who stood about his grave. As his body was lowered they felt that with their beloved general they were burying their last hope for New France.

Wolfe's body was embalmed and taken to England and buried in Westminster Abbey. The spot where he died is marked by a tall column on which are the words, "Here Wolfe died victorious, September 13, 1759."

When the news reached England there was great joy for the victory. Bonfires blazed, bells rang, and triumphant processions marched through the streets to the strains of martial music. But there was one sad spot where all was silent. It was the home of Wolfe's mother. He was a hero now, but he could never come to her again. England respected her grief, and all about her was hushed rejoicing for the victory which had taken his life.

In Quebec there now stands a monument to the honor of Montcalm and Wolfe. Thus is the memory of these two generals united, as united now in Canada are the sons of France and England.

Part 2
Canada under British Rule

Pontiac, Ottawa Chief

Chapter 7
The British in Command

British Rule and Chief Pontiac (1763-1764)
After Wolfe's great victory the French flag came down and the British flag went up. And so, two centuries and a quarter after Cartier first placed the *fleur-de-lis* on Canadian soil, it ceased to wave over that land.

The guarding of the citadel was now the work of the British soldiers. They began at once to put things in order in Quebec, so that they could keep the French soldiers from taking it again. There was so much to be done that they could not stop work even when the coldest weather came, though they suffered greatly, for their clothes were not warm enough for the Canadian winter. They had to keep great fires burning in the guardrooms and barracks, and often, instead of walking through the streets, they ran to keep warm. But even so there were many frozen ears, feet, and hands that first winter.

The good nuns felt so sorry for the Scottish Highlanders, whose kilts did not quite cover their legs, that they knitted them long hose which came up over their knees. The Highlanders were very glad to get them, and in return brought wood for the nuns to burn. There were times when the British soldiers even shared their food with poor Frenchmen. By this you will see that the conquerors were on very friendly terms with the people they had conquered. And so in receiving and returning kindnesses the winter passed by.

Soon after, in the year 1763, a peace was made between France and Britain called the Peace of Paris, which gave Canada formally to Britain. This meant that France would not try to take Canada back again.

The British were so good to the Canadians that they did not object to living under British government. "Military rule" it was called, because the British general in Canada was at the head of affairs. He divided the colony into three parts—Quebec, Three Rivers, and Montreal—and placed a military officer over each. The laws were kept very much as they had been under French rule; and the people were not asked to speak English, but were allowed to keep the French language and the Catholic religion. The habitants in their coarse homespun clothes, brightened by the gay sash or kerchief they liked to wear, cared for their farms and visited their neighbors, and the seigneurs in their large homes gave dinners and parties just as they had done before. All was very much as it had been before the capture of Quebec.

But while the Canadians were living peacefully under the British flag, the First Nations who had been friends with the French were by no means pleased. They did not like the British as well as the French. They missed the warm welcome of the French. There had been old French houses where they had been free to wander at any time, and where no one was ever surprised to see a group of Indigenous people sitting about in the hall. At the fort the French soldiers and officers had received them with honor, and had paid great attention to their wampum belts, feasts, councils, and speeches.

Now all this was changed. The British had no time to spend with them, and let them see that they were not wanted. Even the chiefs received no notice, and the presents which the French had always given them they now very seldom received.

Far from Quebec they had their troubles too. British settlers were going into the First Nations' lands, and British fur traders

British in Command

were travelling wherever they pleased. The First Nations felt they were being treated as if they had no rights in their own land, and they longed for the return of the good old days when the French ruled Canada.

At this time there lived an Algonquin chief, named **Pontiac** (1720–1769), who had great power over his people. When he saw how his people were being treated by the British, he feared that the time might come when they would be driven further and further back from their lands. So he determined to gather the First Nations together to drive away the British and hold Canada for France. He thought he would succeed in this, for he had no idea how powerful the British were.

The French fur traders, to encourage him, told him what was not true. They told him that the French and First Nations together could easily drive the "English dogs" back once more behind the Allegheny Mountains, and that the King of France was sending armies from France to help them.

Pontiac made haste to send about among the First Nations the purple wampum belt and the blood-red tomahawk. These were the signs of war, and the chiefs took them up to show that they were ready to fight with Pontiac.

The great chief made a plan by which he meant to take Fort Detroit. He and his chiefs were to go to the fort and ask for a meeting. Under their blankets they were to carry their guns, cut short so that they could not be seen. When Pontiac was speaking he was to make a sign with a wampum belt which was to be the signal for his warriors to fall upon the British.

Now it happened that a girl from one of the Indigenous tribes wanted to save the life of a British officer at Detroit, and as she could think of no other way, she went and told him all about Pontiac's plan. So when the great chief arrived one bright May morning the British were prepared. The soldiers were in line and every man was armed. When Pontiac saw this, he pretended he loved the English, and said he had just come to "smoke the peace pipe with his English brothers." But he was very angry because his plot had been found out, and a few days later he attacked the fort and besieged it for months. Pontiac did not give up until a strong force came to defend Detroit.

Other forts were taken by the First Nations and destroyed, and the soldiers in them were killed or made prisoners. Fort Michilimackinac, away up on Lake Huron, near the pretty Mackinac Island, was taken by a plot similar to the one which was planned for Detroit. On June 4, King George's birthday, the First Nations asked the officers and soldiers of the fort to go out and watch them play a game of lacrosse in honor of the king. The invitation was gladly accepted, and, not suspecting danger, the British soldiers went out unarmed, leaving the gates open. First Nations women wrapped in blankets wandered in, but the officers were too much interested in the game to wonder why they wore their blankets on such a hot day. Neither did they notice that the game was being played nearer and nearer the walls of the forts until a First Nations man sent the ball to the very gate. The others hurried after it. Then with one piercing war-cry they rushed through the open gate and were inside the palisades. The soldiers now saw that the women wore blankets because they had weapons hidden under them, which they now handed to their men.

The First Nations warriors seized the weapons and fell upon the unarmed soldiers, until they had killed or taken prisoners all who were there. One man, a fur trader named Henry, they did not get. He had not gone out to watch the game. He was busy writing letters that day, and stayed inside the fort. When, after a time, he looked out to see how the game was progressing he was horrified to see his comrades lying dead upon the ground. He knew what had happened, and made his escape to the woods.

To defeat Pontiac and his warriors, two armies had to be sent out. At last the great chief was brought to make peace with the British, and with him surrendered all the tribes that were unfriendly to the British. The war of Pontiac is remarkable because of the careful planning and perseverance which the chief and his men undertook.

Battle of Bushy Run by C.W. Jeffreys (1869–1951), depicting a battle during Pontiac's War

Sir Guy Carleton

Sir Guy Carleton (1724–1808) was the second governor in Canada after the capture of Quebec. From the first he took a great interest in the French-Canadians. He saw that if they were made to feel at home under British rule they would be loyal subjects, and in time of war would defend the British flag.

Because he wished to please them, he did all he could to have the Quebec Act passed. It was an Act which gave his people a governor and a council, and made the laws very much what they had been under royal government. It came into effect in 1774. The French-Canadians were quite content under this form of British rule, for it was like the government they had had under the *fleur-de-lis*.

Sir Guy Carleton was a brave, wise governor, and something happened while he was in Canada which showed how brave and wise he was.

To understand it all we must go over to the English colonies along the sea-coast to the south. During these years they had been growing and prospering so much that the people were beginning to feel that they could take care of themselves without any help from Britain. Besides, they were not altogether pleased with the Quebec Act. They said the laws were made to suit the French and not the English.

While they were feeling this way, Britain passed some acts they did not like. One was an act which made them pay a tax on their tea, the tax-money going to help to pay what Britain had spent in fighting for them against the French.

They were very angry at this. They declared it was unfair, and when a shipload of taxed tea came in to them they had what was called the "Boston Tea Party." This was not a party where people go and drink tea, and talk pleasantly and have a good time. It was no ordinary tea-party, and the people who went to it drank no tea at all. What they did do was to dress themselves up to look like Native Americans and board that British ship and throw all the tea into the water.

British in Command

The British were indignant at such conduct, and closed the port of Boston. After this there was war. That is why one spring day in 1775 the English colonies were all astir. The men were preparing their arms and beating their drums, and the women were weeping and bidding them good-bye, for they were going away to fight against England.

One of the first things they did was to ask Canada to join them. Canada would do nothing of the kind. The French-Canadians liked their governor and liked their laws, and preferred to remain as they were. Sir Guy was right when he said that in time of war they would defend the British flag. And now that time was near.

The people who were going to war in the English colonies said they would make Canada join them, and they sent a large army under the leadership of **Richard Montgomery** (1738–1775) to take Canada.

Sir Guy Carleton was in Montreal when he heard of Montgomery's approach. He knew he was not strong enough to oppose such a great army there, and that he could hope to defend Canada only from the rock-bound citadel of Quebec. But how was he to get there at such a time?

The enemy were all about, and they well knew that if they could only get Sir Guy and keep him prisoner till the war was over they would have but little trouble in taking Canada.

The governor made his plans with the greatest care. Dressed as a fisherman he set out with a few trusted officers in a small boat one dark November night. For provisions they were supplied with only a few biscuits each. All in the little boat knew the risk they ran, and knew too that on the success of their journey hung Canada's fate. The oars were muffled. No word was spoken. Sir

Guy gave his orders by touching the shoulder of the officer nearest him and making a sign. The sign in the same way was passed along.

At Sorel the danger was so great that they barely escaped. The river was bright with the camp fires of the enemy. The men used only the palm of the hand to row with or let the boat move slowly with the water that it might be taken for floating timber.

By the time they reached Three Rivers they were too tired to go further without rest, so they landed and went to an inn. The governor was so weary that he fell asleep with his head resting upon his hands. Suddenly one of his men heard voices that aroused his suspicions. He listened. The voices were those of the enemy's scouts, and they were in the very house where the governor was resting. The man who had heard crossed the room to the sleeping governor and touched him on the shoulder. "Come, come," he said, "it is time we were going."

Sir Guy understood and rose at once. They passed out unnoticed, reached their skiff, and soon were once more on their way down the river. No one at the little inn suspected that one of the weary fishermen who had stopped there to rest was the Governor of Canada.

At last the dangerous trip was over. On the night of November 19, the governor reached the citadel in safety. He was very weary after the long journey, but he took no time to rest, for there was much to be done. He had only about sixteen hundred men, but they were all loyal and true.

The first force of the enemy that arrived called upon Sir Guy to surrender. Sir Guy replied by firing his cannon. Then the enemy withdrew to the Plains of Abraham to think matters over. Soon Montgomery with more soldiers joined them, and then the real work of the brave defenders of Quebec began. Montgomery

British in Command

had been very successful, and he wished to complete his good fortune by taking the citadel. All through December he was on the watch to make Sir Guy surrender. But Sir Guy would not talk with him, for he said, "They are rebels to the British flag."

When Montgomery saw how little good his siege was doing he made an attack. This was done on New Year's morn before daybreak. It had been a dark, stormy night, and in Quebec there was the greatest anxiety, for all felt that the enemy would take advantage of the blinding storm, and that something would be done before morning. The brave men watched the old year out and the new year in, prepared to defend their fortress.

The plan of the enemy was to try to get into Quebec at three different places. They thought the Canadians could not defend so many parts of the citadel at once. They were greatly mistaken, for the Canadians were on the watch everywhere, and drove them back when they attempted to enter the city.

Montgomery had felt very sure of getting into Quebec, for he himself led some soldiers along a narrow path which was quite dark, and which he believed was not carefully guarded. But they had not gone far when, to their surprise, a cannon was fired. Montgomery and several others were killed. Strange to say, he was an old friend of Sir Guy Carleton, and had fought with him under Wolfe at the capture of Quebec. Sir Guy had his body carried into Quebec and buried next day.

The enemy remained encamped about Quebec until May, when they heard that British ships were coming. Then they went away in such a hurry that their general did not even wait to eat his dinner which had been brought to him.

Sir Guy Carleton had saved Canada. The last siege of Quebec was over, and the British flag was left waving where it will wave so long as a Canadian is left to defend it.

Though the people of the English colonies failed to take Canada, they were successful in defeating the British army in their own country. So they took down the British flag and raised the Stars and Stripes, for they were no longer a British colony but an independent republic—the United States of America.

Sir Guy Carleton

Monument remembering United Empire Loyalists in Hamilton, Ontario

Chapter 8
The Loyalists, and a New Province

The United Empire Loyalists

It was not all the people of the New England colonies who fought against Britain in the war that is called the American Revolution. Those who would not join the war and remained loyal to Britain have ever since been called United Empire Loyalists, which means those who were loyal to the British Empire.

The Revolutionaries thought they should help them to fight in their war against Britain, and because they would not do so they ill-treated them in many ways. They even burned their houses and carried off their goods, and when the war was over they would not let them live in peace in their homes. Indeed, there were many who had no homes left to live in. The Loyalists no longer felt safe in that country, for they never knew at what moment they might be attacked or have some serious injury done to them. It is no wonder they determined to leave and come to Canada.

Upon hearing of their trouble Sir Guy Carleton did all he could to help them. The British Government also helped them by giving them farms in Canada and for three years supplying them with food and farm implements.

During the years 1783 and 1784 the greatest number of Loyalists crossed the border. Some went eastward and settled in Nova Scotia and Prince Edward Island, some settled in Quebec, and others went westward to what is now the province of Ontario.

A large number of those who went east formed a settlement at the mouth of the St. John River. It is said that five thousand

Loyalists arrived there in the summer of 1783. This was the beginning of the city of St. John, now our well-known winter harbor. It was also the beginning of the province of New Brunswick. Until this time that territory had belonged to Nova Scotia. When the Loyalists settled there they wished to be represented in the government at Halifax. When this was refused they asked for a division of the province, so that they might have their own parliament. This request was granted. In the year 1784 the Province of New Brunswick was formed, and Colonel Thomas Carleton, a brother of Sir Guy Carleton, was made its governor.

The Loyalists who settled in Nova Scotia, New Brunswick, and Prince Edward Island could go to their new homes by boat from New York. But those who went westward into what is now Ontario had a long and hard journey. Though they could go part of the way by canoe, they had to travel hundreds of miles on horseback or on foot, carrying the treasures that had been spared from their old homes.

The journey was but the beginning of their hardships. Going into Ontario in those days was like going into a wilderness. The Loyalists, many of whom had been used to beautiful homes and servants to wait upon them, must now begin unaided the hard work of chopping down the forest trees and building the little log houses that were to shelter them from the cold and snow. Little boys who had never worked before went to help their fathers in the woods, and little girls gave up their play-hours to help to prepare the noonday meal.

Having no shingles for their little log houses, the Loyalists made the roof of a layer of poles covered with bark, and they filled the cracks with moss and clay to keep out the cold and wet. Chimneys they at first made of sticks and clay, but these were not strong, and were often blown down. The Loyalists became so

The Loyalists, and a New Province

tired of building them up after every windy night that they began to build them of stone. Made in this way, they stood for many years.

The men were so busy clearing the land and planting crops that they had not much time to make furniture. In some of the homes there was only a rough homemade table, and a bed made of poles and basswood bark. Many a little child in those days had only a heap of cedar boughs to sleep upon.

Some of these people were not used to farming, and their crops did not always turn out as they hoped. The year 1788 is called the Hungry Year in what is now Ontario. It was the first year in which the Government did not supply them with food, and the crops in many parts were a failure. There were no stores where they could buy food, nor had they money to buy it with. Some of them sold great portions of land for a little flour. The children gathered the beechnuts, not for Halloween frolics as they do now, but that they might keep the family from starving. Even dried-up roots were carefully gathered from the ground.

There was plenty of game, pigeons and wild turkeys being especially numerous, but the Loyalists had no powder or shot. Hungry men and boys would try all day to kill a partridge, or to catch a fish with some awkward contrivance they had made for the purpose. Usually they went home empty handed.

The Loyalists were kind to one another, and many times would give to a more needy family what they knew they would soon be in want of themselves. A beef bone would sometimes be passed round from house to house, and at each house boiled in the soup "to give it taste." But even then it could not have been very tasty, for they had no salt to put in it.

During this Hungry Year some died of starvation, and some died from eating poisonous roots by mistake. How endless that winter must have seemed, and how they must have longed with all their hearts for another summer! At last it came, bringing to the glad colonists abundant crops. They could not even wait for the grain to ripen, but went to the fields and gathered the green heads of barley, oats, and wheat, grateful that at last there was something to keep them from starvation. The worst of their trials were over now, and real progress began in that part of Canada.

Although the little log houses were far apart, there were many gatherings of the people. The Loyalists became used to travelling the rough roads or following the "blazed trees." In those days where there were no roads they blazed the trees by cutting off pieces of bark, so that the trees thus marked would serve as a guide from clearing to clearing.

The gatherings were not all for pleasure. The Loyalists saw the benefit of working together, and when one man had a large piece of work to do, he would have a "bee" or a "frolic." Down in Nova Scotia they called them "frolics," but in Western Canada they were called "bees," and that name has been kept up ever since.

As the years went by the farmers had larger houses and food in plenty. They could then have a gay feast at their "bees." For some time they did not have much pork or mutton; it was usually the wolves that dined on that. Wild animals were less afraid of man then than in after years, and would stay about the clearings watching for a chance to carry off a luckless lamb or pig. But there was plenty of deer, and wild turkeys, and as the Loyalists had guns now they were able to hunt. They had wild fruit too, and, what the children liked best, maple sugar. So many tall maples grew in Canada that when the Loyalists found out how to make sugar from the sap they had enough for all their needs.

The Loyalists, and a New Province

Their clothing was very plain. At first some had gay clothes brought from the old home, but these were soon worn out. During their first years in Canada the wolves ate so many of their sheep that they had not much wool, but they raised flax and hemp, and out of this they wove coarse cloth. Still there were times when some had nothing but deerskin clothes. The story has come down to us of a young girl who washed her deerskin dress in lye. As soap was scarce the Loyalists used this to wash their linen. But it did not do for the deerskin, as the young lady found, for her garment shriveled up before her eyes, and she could wear it no more. As it was the only one she had, she was obliged to wrap herself in a blanket, in the Indigenous fashion, until another dress could be made for her.

They had not many dishes at first either, and most of those they had were made of wood. It was no uncommon thing for them to carry their dishes with them to a "bee," lest the hostess might not have enough.

The "Yankee peddlers" went among them with dishes, calicoes, and muslins, but the price was so dear that very few could afford to buy. Still they were always glad to look at the things. It was a great day in the lonely settler's home when the peddler stopped before the door and opened his pack. Sometimes a muslin wedding dress was bought, but many a young bride wore only a deerskin dress and a squirrel-skin bonnet when she followed the blazed trees to the new log house that was to be her future home.

Such were the early days of the Loyalists who went to the forests, endured the hardships of such a life, paved the way for other settlers, and did so much towards the building up of Canada.

Joseph Brant

Many of the First Nations were loyal to Britain during this Revolution, and have an equal right to the name United Empire Loyalists.

It must not be forgotten that one of the most notable of the Loyalists was a handsome Mohawk chief, **Joseph Brant** (1743-1807), or Thayendanegea, as his tribe called him.

He was always on the side of the English. When only a boy of about thirteen years of age he fought under Sir William Johnson, one of the English generals, in the war between the French and English in Canada. Sir William was greatly pleased with the bright boy, and, after the capture of Quebec, he sent him to school, where he made such rapid progress that a missionary among the Mohawks selected him as his interpreter. Later when the Pontiac War broke out he joined a company against the Algonquin leader who was trying to overthrow British rule in Canada. In his warfare Brant was always most humane, and did what he could to save the prisoners from torture and death.

Joseph Brant was honored both by the First Nations and the Europeans. A well-known minister said of him, "He behaved so much like a Christian and a soldier that he won great esteem." The First Nations honored him by making him the Great Chief of the Six Nations—the Mohawks, the Senecas, the Oneidas, the Cayugas, the Onondagas, and the Tuscaroras. Each of these tribes had its chief, but Joseph Brant was the supreme chief over all.

The Loyalists, and a New Province

Joseph Brant

During the American Revolution he fought loyally for Britain. When it was over he was homeless; the Mohawk valley where he lived had been laid waste. Though the Senecas offered him a home with them, he preferred to bring his people to Canada and live under the British flag.

They settled on the banks of the Grand River, where grants of land were given to them by the British Government, very much as they had been given to the white Loyalist settlers. But there was one difference: the First Nations were not allowed to sell their land. The county of Brant where they settled was named from their chief.

After this Brant went on a visit to England, in order to induce those in authority there to take more interest in his people. He was received with great honor, listened to with much attention, and was introduced to the king.

While in England he was invited to a fancy-dress ball. The great chief went in his costume of a Mohawk warrior, with gay paint, feathers in his head-dress, and a tomahawk in his belt, and wore no mask. One of the guests, taking the handsome dark face for a mask, touched his nose. Now the great chief was in a playful mood. He waved his tomahawk over the head of the startled Englishman, and at the same time gave the Mohawk war-cry. Never before had such a sound resounded through an English ballroom. Some of the guests were alarmed, and would have left the room had they not been told what it meant. The inquisitive guest knew now without a doubt that it was no masked Englishman whose nose he had taken the liberty of tapping, but a real Mohawk chief.

At his new home on the Grand River, Joseph Brant had a church built for his people, which was the first church in Ontario. The great chief himself translated the Gospel of St. Mark and the Church of England Prayer Book into the Mohawk language. He also attended to much public business, which, as one man said of him, "required energy, wisdom, and a cultivated mind."

Joseph Brant loved his people with all his heart. His last words were, "Have pity upon the poor Indians; if you can get any influence with the great, endeavour to do them all the good you can." In the city of Brantford a beautiful monument was erected to the memory of this famous United Empire Loyalist.

Governor Simcoe

"Deyonguhokrawen" is a long word, as many First Nations words are, but then it means so much. We could not express it in one word in English. We should have to use six, for we must say, "One whose door is always open."

That is what they called **Governor John Graves Simcoe** (1752–1806) because he always made them welcome, no matter

The Loyalists, and a New Province

how often they came or how long they stayed. He became a great favorite with the First Nations men, who like to go early and stay late.

He was the first governor of Ontario, though the province was not called Ontario at that time, but Upper Canada. What is now the province of Quebec was called Lower Canada.

Before this all the country was governed by the same laws, but a great change had to be made when the Loyalists came to live there. They did not at all like the laws the French were ruled by. Sir Guy Carleton wanted to please them and to please the French, and the British Parliament wanted to please both Loyalists and French-Canadians. So to do this the Constitutional Act was passed, which formed the two provinces and gave a governor and a parliament to each.

Governor Simcoe

This was considered a very wise arrangement at the time, as Upper Canada, settled by the Loyalists, could have different laws from Lower Canada, where the French lived. You have all heard of the Parliament Buildings at Ottawa. Some of you have seen them, others have seen pictures of them. There were no such fine buildings as that for the Loyalists. The first Parliament House was a little log building, so tiny that you might have to travel a long way in some parts of Ontario today before you would find a house so small. It was situated at Newark, afterwards called Niagara, which, though only a group of little houses, was the first capital of Upper Canada.

But, though it was so small, Governor Simcoe was not at all ashamed of it, and one September day in 1792 he opened his Parliament with as much pride and dignity as if the building were very grand, and the country, instead of a stretch of forest with a few small clearings, a land of fine farms and large cities. He knew it would be like that someday.

The members had a hard time to reach the log Parliament building. They did not go in fast cars, as they do nowadays. Some came long distances through the woods on foot, many came part of the way in canoes and walked the rest, a few more fortunate ones had ridden on horseback.

The governor called his headquarters Navy Hall, and wrote that name on the letters he sent home to England. His friends far across the ocean had no idea that it was but a small building in a tiny village surrounded by forests, and that bears and wolves prowled about at night, and even in broad daylight had been known to walk down Main Street.

Governor Simcoe's little boy was a great pet in the tiny settlement. His name was Francis, but the First Nations called him

The Loyalists, and a New Province

Tioga, meaning "the swift." To please them the governor always dressed him up in deerskins on State occasions.

Before long the governor decided that Newark was not a good place for the capital of Upper Canada. He said it should be nearer the centre of the province and farther away from the United States. So he set out to find a more suitable spot.

He crossed Lake Ontario, and came to a place which he saw would make an excellent harbor. Here he moved his Parliament. It is where Toronto now stands, and has been the capital of the province ever since. They called it Little York then, sometimes Muddy York, because the land there was so marshy. Long before this the First Nations had named that spot Toronto, meaning "trees in water."

After it grew to be a big place and the marshy land was drained, it was no longer right to call it either Little York or Muddy York, so they gave the capital its pretty name which it still has today, Toronto.

When Governor Simcoe first went there he had no house to live in, but stayed in a canvas tent. He would not keep the people waiting for their ball on that account, but gave it in the tent. No doubt it was just as gay an occasion as any ball since.

The builders were good workmen, and it was not long before Governor Simcoe could move out of his tent into his new house. He named it Castle Frank, after Francis, his little son. It was a large building for those days, made of logs with plenty of nail heads to be seen. As it had a great chimney in the centre and many trees about, it made a quaint picture from the river.

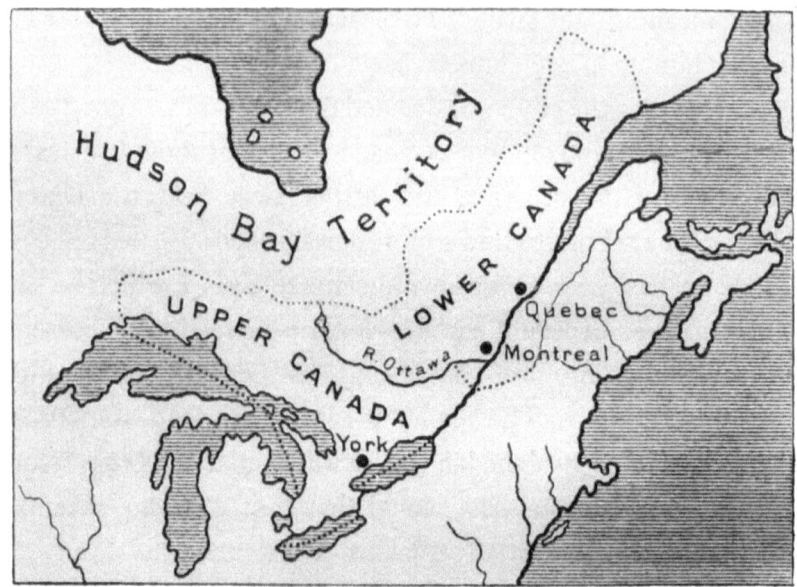

Governor Simcoe travelled on horseback over much of the country, and did all he could to open up the province. Seeing how hard it was for the people to travel by land, he had roads made. He laid out what are to this day two of our main travelled highways, Yonge Street from Toronto to Lake Simcoe, and Dundas Street from Toronto to London.

He also had a number of gunboats on Lake Ontario, and was arranging to have some on Lake Erie. This he hoped would be the beginning of a Royal Navy in Canada. Governor Simcoe did not remain in Canada long enough to see the completion of his work. In the year 1796 he was recalled, and sent to govern the island of St. Domingo.

It may be of interest to remember that the legend upon Simcoe's family coat-of-arms was "*Non sibi sed patriae*," "not for himself but for his country." His work in Canada proved that he had made it his motto.

The Loyalists, and a New Province

The same year that Governor Simcoe went to St. Domingo, Canada also lost Sir Guy Carleton (or Lord Dorchester as he had been made), who for years had labored for the interests of Canada and of both her French- and English-speaking subjects.

Chapter 9
The War of 1812

Sir Isaac Brock

Major-General **Sir Isaac Brock** (1769–1812) was one of Canada's great heroes. It was well for Canadians that he was with them in the year 1812, for their country was in danger and sadly in need of such a hero.

The people of the United States were causing trouble. They were going to invade Canada again. They were feeling very sure of success, too, for Britain was at war with France, and could not spare many soldiers or guns to her colony in the New World. General Brock discovered that they were making preparations for war, so he made preparations too. Though Canada was only a weak country compared with the United States, her population being only about one-fifteenth as great, he did not despair.

He felt that he could depend upon the Canadians, and he was right. They left their farms or their shops under the charge of their wives, sisters, or daughters, and joined the ranks. Though the danger was great, they were brave and true, and found faithful helpers among the First Nations.

Sir Isaac Brock

In the month of July, a United States general came over to Canada and told the Canadians that they would be much better off living under the flag of the United States. He said that if they stayed at home while the United States army drove away the few British soldiers, tore down the Union Jack, and put up the Stars and Stripes, they should be kindly treated; but that if they refused to give themselves up to the United States, the horrors of war would be upon them.

At this the Canadians were indignant. Sir Isaac Brock made a speech in which he said that they would teach the enemy a lesson. They would teach them that "a country defended by free men devoted to the cause of their king and their constitution cannot be conquered."

And his people said, "We will defend our country and our flag. Though they outnumber us, they shall not conquer us."

In October of that same year was fought the great battle of Queenston Heights. Queenston is situated on a high plateau on

The War of 1812

the bank of the Niagara River. It was a natural Canadian stronghold, the Quebec of Upper Canada.

Just opposite, on the United States side, a large army was stationed. Sir Isaac Brock had been watching this army carefully, and making ready for the attack he felt sure would come. One October morning the Niagara River was beautiful in the dim morning light, and the trees on either side were tinted with the bright shades of autumn. Soon it was to be a scene of bloodshed and death.

Before daybreak the United States soldiers were crossing the river. The sound of their oars aroused the watchful Canadians, who fired upon them. Although some were wounded, about thirteen hundred managed to land. One of their captains led part of them up the steep rock by a fisherman's path that was supposed to be impassable and not guarded. As soon as they gained the crest, the fight began. Brock was not at Queenston at the time. He had spent the night at Fort George, a few miles away. As was his custom, he had risen before daylight that morning. Little did he know it was to be his last morning on earth. Hearing the cannon in the distance, he called for his horse and galloped to Queenston. Before he reached it, he saw that an attack was being made. As he hurried up the hill, he called out, "Follow me, boys;" and waving his sword, he shouted, "Push on, the brave York Volunteers." He had given his last command. Scarcely had he finished speaking when he fell, struck by a ball from an enemy's gun. An officer hurried to his side, but he was dying. With his last breath he asked that his death should be kept from his men. His body was carried to a house nearby, and the fight went on.

All was well ordered, for the wise directions he had given in case of attack were carefully followed. The Canadians fought furiously. The enemy were now in a dangerous position. The steep precipice and the Niagara River were on one side, and on the other were Canada's gallant defenders. Though they fired their most deadly volleys they failed to check the advance of the Canadians. Seeing that it was useless to fight longer, the United States officers raised the white flag, and the battle of Queenston Heights was won.

The death of Brock made it a dearly-bought victory for Canada. In all loyal hearts that day joy was mingled with sorrow—joy for the victory, sorrow for the great loss which had been its price.

As soon as the fighting was over, Brock's body was carried to Newark, and on October 16 buried at Fort George, where he had spent the last night of his life.

On Queenston Heights there now stands a monument in memory of this heroic general, and on the spot where he fell our late king, Edward the Seventh, when on a visit to Canada as Prince of Wales, placed a stone. Far away in London, England, in St. Paul's Cathedral there is a monument, and on it is carved the dying general in the arms of an officer, a grief-stricken First Nations warrior standing near.

Though the Canadians won the battle of Queenston Heights, the war was by no means over. It was more than two years before the people of the United States gave up trying to take Canada.

The War of 1812

Tecumseh

Amongst the First Nations who helped the Canadians in this war was a great chief named **Tecumseh** (1768–1813). He was a fine-looking man, with clear bright eyes that seemed to see everything. Suspended from his nose he wore three small crowns. He also wore a silver medallion of George the Third, of which he was very proud and kept fastened to a string of wampum that he wore around his neck. His moccasins were gay indeed, for they were trimmed with porcupine quills dyed in brilliant colors.

His tribesmen loved and admired him, and followed him willingly. He had great power over them, and kept them from scalping or ill-treating their captives. Tecumseh had once lived in the United States, but the people there had not treated him well, so he came to Canada, and was very glad to help to drive back the invaders.

Tecumseh

When he met General Brock, he told him that his allies were ready to shed their last drop of blood in the service of their "great father," the King of England. General Brock was greatly pleased with him, and felt that he could be trusted in every way.

He asked Tecumseh for information about some part of the country round Detroit. The clever man laid a piece of birch bark upon the ground, placed a stone at each end to keep it down, and made a drawing upon it with his knife, showing hills, rivers, and roads. It was an excellent map when finished, and of great use to General Brock, who soon after made the United States army at Detroit surrender.

Tecumseh died fighting for Canada. The year after the victory of Queenston Heights he was killed in the battle of Moraviantown. Early in October one of Canada's armies was marching to Burlington Heights. Tecumseh and five hundred of his warriors were with them. A large United States army which was following them overtook them at Moraviantown, a First Nation settlement on the Thames River.

Tecumseh chose the battleground. Wisely he picked a spot where the Thames River was on one side and a swamp on the other, and they could be attacked only in front. The warriors took up their position in the swamp. "Father, have a big heart," said Tecumseh to the general, as he left him to join his own warriors. Little did they think it was the last time he would lead them in battle.

Stealthily the enemy advanced, keeping out of sight as much as possible by hiding behind trees, until quite near. Then with a rush they were upon the waiting army. The men were tired after their long tramp. They seemed to have little confidence in their leader, and the charge of the enemy frightened them. Almost as soon as the battle began they broke from the ranks, their leader with them, and fled to Burlington.

It was Tecumseh and his Indigenous followers who bravely stood their ground, and fought for the British flag after the Europeans had given up the day. But against the great army they could do nothing. Tecumseh was shot. His son, a boy of seventeen, was near him at the time and saw him fall, but fought bravely on. It was all in vain.

After the victors had marched away, and the battlefield was lonely and still, the friends of Tecumseh, those who had the best right to all that remained, found his body, and buried it we know not where.

True Canadians will always think with the deepest gratitude of what Tecumseh did for the country in those days when her peril was so great.

Laura Secord
There was a female hero in this war, and because of the brave deed she did a victory was won for Canada.

At Beaver Dams, not far from where St. Catherines now stands, **Colonel James Fitzgibbon** (1780–1863) was stationed with some soldiers and First Nations. A United States army meant to surprise and capture Fitzgibbon's little band.

Now it happened that a couple of United States officers wandered into James Secord's little house one day and demanded food. **Laura Secord** (1775–1868), his wife, brought them something to eat. While enjoying their meal they talked over their plans for capturing Fitzgibbon and his men. They forgot to talk quietly, and never guessed that Mrs. Secord heard it all.

Laura Secord

As soon as they were gone she told her husband what they had been saying. "We must do something," she exclaimed; "Fitzgibbon must be warned."

James Secord had been wounded in the battle of Queenston Heights, and could do nothing now but stay quietly at home.

"As you cannot go," his wife said, "I must."

At first he was unwilling, but at last, for the sake of his country, he consented. The next morning Laura Secord rose very early, and had everything neat and tidy in her little house. She knew that she must be very careful lest the enemy should learn of her errand, and if an officer should wander in through the day he must not find the house looking as if she had taken a hasty journey.

Laura thought more of getting safely past the pickets of the enemy than of her own comfort. She wanted them to think that she had only gone to milk, so she wore no shoes or stockings and only a short flannel skirt and cotton jacket. As soon as it was day she took a milk-pail in one hand and a milk-stool in the other and drove one of the cows up to the lines of the enemy. She was really driving it on, yet she made it appear to the sentry that she was trying to overtake it and drive it back. "It is a contrary creature," she said when he noticed her.

He suspected nothing and let her go. Once past him she drove the cow on until she was out of sight, when she hastily milked it, hid the pail, and hurried on her way. It was a hot morning, for it was the 23rd of June, and the forest was close and full of flies and mosquitoes. She had to go a long roundabout way for fear of meeting the enemy, and she was often frightened by snakes or wolves or strange sounds in the dense woods, and always in fear of losing her way.

At last the sun set, but Laura travelled on, growing very weary and very much afraid that as night fell she would be lost in the darkness. Soon she came to an opening, where there was a party of First Nations. The chief came to her at once. Laura put aside her fear, and tried her best to make him understand her. She repeated Fitzgibbon's name, and made signs that she wished to be taken to him. She knew that the First Nations called the United States soldiers "big knives," so she pointed to the knife at his belt and made signs to show that there were many "big knives" coming.

It was hard for Laura Secord to get the man to know what she meant, but after she had made signs over and over, he showed his assent. He led her through the fields to a house, where she found Colonel Fitzgibbon. No wonder he was surprised when he saw this small, delicate woman who had travelled from sunrise to sunset through the forests to reach him.

Early the next morning the United States army marched to Beaver Dams, but instead of surprising Fitzgibbon, they found him expecting them. He had made the most of his few men, and his warriors had hidden behind trees, and were keeping up their terrible war-whoops. The United States soldiers thought there must be many more Canadian soldiers and First Nations warriors than there really were, and were easily brought to surrender.

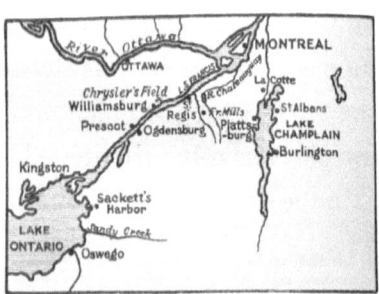

The War of 1812

Other Battles and the Close of the War

Canada won some great victories after the attack at Beaver Dams. Among these was a battle fought on the Chateauguay River and another at Chrysler's Farm. Both of these occurred late in the same year (1813), when two large armies were marching against Montreal. One was going down the St. Lawrence, and the other down the Chateauguay River, and the plan was to meet where these two rivers join and make an attack upon Montreal.

The only hope of the Canadians was to keep the armies from meeting. But how were they to manage it with their small numbers? The story of these two victories will tell. The army that was marching by way of Chateauguay consisted of about three thousand five hundred men. To check their advance a French-Canadian, **Colonel De Salaberry** (1778-1829), led a brave little band of less than four hundred French-Canadians and a few First Nations warriors. The leader threw up his defences in the woods beside the river bank, where there were a number of deep ravines and a swamp on one side. Half a mile farther back was a ford of the river where a small reserve force was stationed. There, hidden away in the forest, they waited until the great invading army came upon them.

At first the little band was driven back, but their leader, De Salaberry, seized his little bugler to keep him from running away, and commanded him to sound the advance call. The reserve force down the river heard that sound and moved forward. Colonel Macdonell, their leader, ordered his buglers to scatter in the woods and make as much noise as possible.

When the enemy heard bugles resounding from far and near they thought the woods must be full of soldiers. The shouting of the Canadians and the whooping of the First Nations helped to alarm them, and, feeling sure that they were facing a large force, they turned and fled.

In this way the battle of Chateauguay was won by less than four hundred men against nearly ten times their number of United States regulars.

As the other army moved down the St. Lawrence, a band of about eight hundred Canadian soldiers followed closely, causing much annoyance to the rear of the invading army.

At Chrysler's Farm the great army of the enemy halted, and turned to "brush away the fly" that had been annoying them. But it happened that "the fly" brushed the great army away. The spot where the invading army chose to wait was in a field, where they were protected by a stone wall and some cliffs. But the little band of Canadians were not alarmed when they saw the position the enemy held. On the contrary, they were in such a hurry to charge that instead of advancing in a dignified, soldierly manner, they ran towards their foe. When their bayonets flashed and their cheers rang out, the enemy, frightened by such spirit, broke their ranks and fled.

So both of these armies were turned back, and Montreal was safe from attack.

Little York, the capital of Upper Canada, had not been so fortunate as Montreal. As it was not a military post, no one supposed that it would be attacked, and the only defences it possessed were some French guns, and some earthworks that the French had made long ago to protect themselves. At this time it was a quiet village of about one thousand inhabitants, and important only because it was the seat of government.

But one day these peaceful villagers were astonished to find themselves surrounded by the enemy. The United States fleet had come across the lake, and a United States army had come by land. All the men of the village who could fight were away at the front. But just at this time one of the Canadian generals with a few soldiers happened to be passing through York. The boys, old men, and even the invalids shouldered their muskets and joined him, making altogether about six hundred. But they could not resist so great a force. Had they tried to do so, they would have been shot down. The general withdrew his men and went on his way, and the little village surrendered on conditions that it should be protected.

The enemy broke this agreement. They burned the Parliament Buildings, carried off the books in the library, and destroyed some of the private houses.

Before the war was over, the Canadian soldiers went over to Washington, the capital of the United States, and burned the Capitol and other public buildings there in retaliation for the burning of the public buildings of York.

While the Canadians had been winning victories by land, they had been less successful on lake and sea. They had not so fine a fleet as the United States, and Britain, while at war with France, could not spare them many war vessels. The United States fleet had control of the Great Lakes, and had also won some victories over the British at sea. But in the summer of 1813 the British won a great sea victory, as you shall hear.

In the month of June the United States frigate, the *Chesapeake*, happened to be in the harbor of Boston when a British ship of war, the *Shannon*, appeared. The *Shannon* was manned by a brave crew, commanded by **Captain Broke**. The captain longed to win a battle that would wipe out the disgrace he felt their defeats at sea had brought upon them. So he sent a challenge to the captain of the *Chesapeake* asking if he might have "the honor of a meeting, to try the fortunes of our flags." Captain Lawrence of the *Chesapeake* gladly consented. The *Chesapeake* had just been refitted in the harbor and made ready for battle, so he felt sure of winning the victory.

When he sailed out to meet his opponent, the people of Boston followed in their pleasure boats to see their captain win the day. But the victory was not to be theirs. As the great ships met, there was a terrific cannonade from both. Almost the moment they came together, the crew of the *Shannon* boarded the *Chesapeake*. Captain Lawrence, while fighting at the head of his men, was mortally wounded. In a quarter of an hour, the flag of the *Chesapeake* came down, and the victory lay with the *Shannon*. When Captain Broke sailed back to port at Halifax, he had the *Chesapeake* in tow. The *Shannon* had won back the name and fame of British ships at sea.

One of the greatest battles of the next year was fought at a roadway near Niagara Falls, called Lundy's Lane. It was a terrible battle, and lasted from five o'clock one hot July afternoon until twelve at night.

The people of the United States were discouraged after this defeat, for they were no nearer conquering Canada than they had been the year before. They knew they would be less likely to succeed now, for the war between Britain and France was over. Britain had defeated Napoleon, the great man who had wanted all Europe for a playground, and whose game had been to dethrone kings and put others in their places. She had shipped him off to a lonely island, where he could do no harm. Having no longer to fear him, she could spare help to her colony. There was nothing for the United States soldiers to do but go home defeated.

On Christmas Day, 1814, peace was made. The Canadians were glad to know that there was to be no more bloodshed. It had been a hard three years for them.

The War of 1812

The people of the United States have never since attempted to invade Canada. They had learned the lesson General Brock said Canadians would teach them "That a country defended by free men devoted to the cause of their king and their constitution cannot be conquered."

Canadians had learned that their people, no matter what language they spoke or from what country they came, were as one in their defense of their country and their flag.

William Lyon Mackenzie

Chapter 10
A Rebellion and What Became of It

Mackenzie and the Rebellion

When the war of 1812 was over, and there was no longer danger from an enemy, the Canadians had time to think about their home troubles. You read some time ago that the Constitutional Act gave Upper and Lower Canada each a governor and a council.

Now the great trouble was that the governor and council were managing everything in their own way, and were spending the money of the country as they thought best, and not as the people wished. The councillors held their position for life; so when they began doing what they ought not to do the people could not get them out of office, but had to be ruled by them and obey the laws even if they were unjust.

There was an Assembly to which the people could send members, and they could change them every four years if they wished, as we now do our members of Parliament. But the members of the Assembly could not do much, for the councillors saw that they had no power.

The Constitutional Act had seemed a wise form of government at first, but times had changed. Canadians now wanted to have some voice in making their laws. Living and working in Canada, they knew better what they needed than the men who were sent over from England to govern them.

The governor and councillors did not mean to do wrong, but they could not understand that what had suited Canada years ago was not good for her now that her population was so much greater and her people better educated. The Home Government in England, too, did not realize that Canada should be treated as a grown-up country.

At this time there was no such wise governor as Sir Guy Carleton to keep matters right, or perhaps the trouble this story tells of might have been prevented.

Those who wanted changes or reforms in the government were called Reformers. In Upper Canada the councillors were all friends, and thought alike just as if they were members of the same family, so they were called the Family Compact.

The Reform Party in Lower Canada had an able leader in Louis Joseph Papineau. He was a French-Canadian, who had been Speaker in the Assembly in Lower Canada for many years.

One of the Reformers in Upper Canada who did most talking about the affairs of the country was a little Scotsman named **William Lyon Mackenzie** (1795–1861). He owned a newspaper, and so he could print what he said. He published the wrongdoings of the Family Compact, and made so many sharp remarks about them, which they usually deserved, that he was called the "peppery little Scotsman." When his enemies wished to be very scornful they would say, "that little mannikin from York."

Fifteen young men, friends of the Family Compact, declared they would put a stop to his paper. They broke into his office one night when he was away, carried off his printing-press, and threw it into the lake. They soon found that this would not stop Mackenzie. He sued for damages, took the money thus obtained, bought a new press, and continued his paper. But all that he could say was of no avail; the Family Compact would have their way.

Then the people wrote about their troubles to the Home Government; but this, too, was useless, for the councillors took care that the Home Government had their side of the story first.

A Rebellion

Mackenzie and many others made up their minds that the only thing to do was to fight for the right to manage their own affairs. So it happened that Mackenzie led a rebellion in Upper Canada, while **Louis-Joseph Papineau** (1786–1871) was at the head of those in Lower Canada who were rising in protest against the Government.

The trained soldiers were on the side of the Government, and the men who followed Mackenzie and Papineau knew little about fighting. Sometimes they would gather together and practice, usually in some shadowy spot at twilight, for they did not want the Government to know what they were about. As they had only a few guns they fitted pikes into hickory handles to use as weapons.

Late in November of that year there was some fighting in Lower Canada. At St. Denis a band of Papineau's men had collected. Colonel Gore marched against them. One dark stormy night he led his men for sixteen miles over roads that were deep with mud. In the morning he made an attack, but the habitants fought desperately and he was obliged to retreat. At St. Charles another band of Papineau's followers collected and raised what they called a "Liberty Column" in honor of Papineau. Their leader was a man from the United States named Brown. To defeat them a Government army marched through rain and storm over muddy roads and broken bridges, until on the 25th they reached the spot where "General Brown" had taken up his position. At the very beginning of the fight the "pasteboard general" fled, and though the habitants fought bravely they were soon defeated.

At a little village north of Montreal another band had gathered together, but when they heard soldiers were coming a number took refuge in a large four-storied stone church. There they held out bravely, refusing to escape until the roof was blazing and the very walls falling about them.

In Upper Canada the rebels met with no better success. Early in December 1837 they set out to take Toronto, but they did not get so far as that, for soldiers marched out and defeated them four miles from the capital. The Government offered one thousand pounds to anyone who would catch Mackenzie.

But Mackenzie was too smart for them. He got away to the United States in safety, though he had many narrow escapes on the way. At one time he hid in a pig pen, and, looking through a chink, saw men riding about hunting for him. At another time he was taken for a horse thief, and was nearly sent to prison.

Once across the border he gathered his followers together on Navy Island, in the Niagara River, and prepared to invade Canada. They had a little boat, the *Caroline*, which carried food to them from the shore. The Government soldiers, one dark starless night, set her on fire and cut her loose from her moorings. From Navy Island the little band watched the bright light, but not till she drifted near them did they know it was the *Caroline* floating all aflame down the river and over the great falls. After their boat was destroyed they came over to Canada and made an attack, but were defeated. Later a band arrived from the United States to help Mackenzie's cause. They took up their position in a windmill near Prescott on the St. Lawrence. There they held out for three days against the Government soldiers. Their leader and nine of his helpers were afterwards tried and executed. Two men in Upper Canada, Lount and Matthews, were also executed for the part they had taken in the rebellion.

A Rebellion

Lord Durham

When the Home Government heard of the rebellion they felt sure that something must be very wrong, or Canadians would never go so far as to rebel. They sent **Lord Durham** (1792-1840) to Canada to see what really was the trouble, and to find out how matters might be made right.

Lord Durham was far too clever to let the Family Compact talk him over to their way of thinking, though they were anxious enough to do so. He stayed only six months in Canada, but in that short time he saw exactly how matters stood. He saw that the Canadians knew better what laws they needed than the men sent over from England, and he saw that Canada could never grow and prosper until her Government was responsible to the people.

He made out a report of all he learned and sent it to the Home Government. When it was read, Lord Durham's advice was taken. Canada was given what her people had been wanting, responsible government.

An Act of Union was passed, joining Upper and Lower Canada again under one governor and one parliament. The people were given the right to elect the councillors who acted as advisers to the governor, and to put them out of office if they were not doing right. The members of the Assembly elected by the people were given charge of the money. This was a great change from the time of the rebellion, when the councillors were managing everything.

Many stories are told of the rebellion, and from them we may form a clear idea of the trouble it gave those living in the districts where the fighting took place. One of these stories tells of Government soldiers pretending to search for arms in the house of a Reformer, and carrying off a fine pair of boots.

"Why do you let them take your shoes?" said the little girl to her father after they had gone.

"I dare not interfere with anything they do," the father replied.

At another place a little boy was holding his father's horses at the door, when some soldiers commanded him to get into the wagon and drive them to their destination. His mother, who saw it all from the window, was greatly frightened. It was almost dark, the horses were wild, and he had never driven them before, and she feared he would never get back in safety. However, he came back without an accident, though at a late hour.

At one house where the father and son were away fighting for the Government, some Reformers entered and demanded food. They carried off all the meat and bread, leaving the family to live on milk until they could borrow a little flour.

But the men did not always succeed in getting what they wanted, for a story is told of a little girl of ten years who was determined that Mackenzie's men should not be fed at her father's house. Seeing some men on their way in one day, she rolled up two loaves of bread—all the provisions they had—and dropped them out of the window, where they lay hidden by a rosebush until the men were gone.

One morning an old man got up very early and went out to look at the sky to see what sort of a day it was going to be. As he did not mean to go further than his own gate, he had not taken off his red nightcap; but just then some Government soldiers came along and, taking him for one of the rebels, marched him off to Toronto, red nightcap and all.

A Rebellion

Lord Durham

Chapter 11
Responsible Government

Lord Elgin

Had we been in Montreal on a certain night in the year 1849, we might have seen a carriage driven wildly through the streets, with a crowd of men hurling stones and rotten eggs after it. Some large stones are thrown with great force, and we fear they will smash through the carriage and strike those who are in it. But it is drawn by fast horses and soon is out of reach.

We should naturally ask who is in the carriage which they are treating in this way. If we could get an answer from the excited throng we should be told that it is **Lord Elgin** (1811–1863), Governor of Canada.

Lord Elgin

"What has he done to deserve such treatment?" would be our next question.

But they are all hurrying off to the Parliament Buildings, Montreal being at that time the capital of Canada, and it is not likely any one would take time to answer.

We are still more surprised at what has taken place when we learn that Lord Elgin is the son-in-law of Lord Durham, who did so much for Canada, and one of whose last remarks was, "Canadians will one day do justice to my memory."

We know that Canadians remember him with gratitude, and we feel sure that it was only a few who were treating his son-in-law unkindly. It was the friends of the Family Compact, who had never been pleased with the new form of government. They did not like having their power taken away from them, and for that reason they did not want responsible government in Canada. However, this made no difference at all, for the governors, with the exception of one, were determined to rule as the people wished.

When Lord Elgin came something happened which showed the Family Compact very plainly that they could not have their own way. It is interesting to notice that before Lord Elgin ever thought of coming to Canada he wrote, in a letter to Lord Durham's daughter, "The real vindication of Lord Durham's memory and proceedings will be the success of a Governor-general of Canada who works out his views of government fairly. Depend upon it, if this country is governed for a few years satisfactorily, Lord Durham's reputation as a statesman will be raised beyond the reach of cavil."

And now Lord Elgin as Governor-general of Canada was to "work out his views of government fairly," at a time when the country was in a condition of political turmoil. He was to show the people that when the majority wished a certain Bill to be passed, the few could not prevent it.

Responsible Government

The trouble arose when the people made up their minds to pay those who had met with loss because of the rebellion, though they had taken no part in it. A Bill for this purpose, called the Rebellion Losses Bill, was brought up in Parliament. At first the Bill included only Upper Canada, but as the people of Lower Canada protested, and said that their losses too should be paid, the Bill was finally made to include them also.

Now the Family Compact party in Upper Canada declared that the Lower Canadians should not have any money for their losses. They said that all in Lower Canada had been rebels at heart, and that if they had not joined the rebellion it was not because they were opposed to it. Their cry was, "No pay to rebels."

However, the Bill was passed in the legislature and submitted to the Governor-general for his signature. Seeing that the majority wished the Lower Canadians to have their share of the Rebellion Losses money, Lord Elgin signed the Bill.

When those who had opposed the Bill heard what had been done they were angry, and shouts of "Down with Lord Elgin!" rang through the air. Scarcely had the governor left the Parliament Buildings, when an angry mob ran after his carriage throwing stones and rotten eggs at it. As the news spread the mob grew larger. Carrying stones, muskets, and torches they hurried to the Parliament Buildings. They threw stones at the windows, smashed the lamps, overturned the tables, and broke the chairs. Others set the buildings on fire, and soon the whole place was in flames. Someone tried to carry out a picture of Queen Victoria, that had cost twelve thousand dollars, but even that did not escape injury, for at the door a ruffian thrust a stick through the canvas.

Upon reaching home Lord Elgin found on the top of his carriage a stone of two pounds weight that had been hurled at him.

Very wisely he decided not to drive through the streets of Montreal for several days. This was not because he was afraid for his personal safety, but because he did not wish to be attacked, lest he might have to put the mob down by force of arms. At a time when his life was in real danger, he said, "I am prepared to bear any amount of hatred that may be cast upon me, but if I can possibly prevent it, no stain of blood shall rest upon my name."

His enemies asked the Home Government to take him away and send them a new governor, but nothing of the kind was done. Because of his services the British Government raised him to the British peerage under the title of Baron Elgin of Elgin. Until his term of office was up he remained Governor of Canada.

Though the Parliament Buildings were burned and stones thrown at the governor and the Queen's picture injured, some good came out of the turmoil. The Family Compact and their friends learned that, no matter how many stones were thrown or buildings burned, Canada would have responsible government.

Montreal had insulted her governor, and was never the capital again. For a time Parliament was held in Toronto and in Quebec. At last the Queen chose for the purpose Bytown, a little lumbering village prettily situated on the Ottawa River. The name was changed to Ottawa, and it has ever since been the capital of Canada. Our beautiful Dominion Parliament Buildings now stand where years ago only lumbermen lived.

Lemuel Allan Wilmot

There were men in Nova Scotia, New Brunswick, and Prince Edward Island who were trying to gain responsible government for these provinces. But they did not do it by fighting with muskets and pikes fitted into hickory handles. They held meetings, made brilliant speeches, and wrote newspaper articles. In this way they

Responsible Government

succeeded, and it was not long before the provinces down by the sea were given the same rights as Canada.

The man who did the most towards bringing about responsible government in New Brunswick was **Lemuel Allan Wilmot** (1809-1878). He won his chief success by his great talent as a speaker. Once he made a great speech at a convention in the United States. The convention was held for the purpose of trying to arrange for a shorter ocean route to Europe. At that time no one dreamed that before very long they would have boats that could go from New York to Liverpool in less than six days. So they thought of shortening the time then required to cross the ocean by changing the route of their vessels and running them from some port on the west coast of Ireland to a port on the east coast of Nova Scotia, which they would connect with New York by rail. At this meeting some of the greatest speakers of the United States and Canada had gathered, but by far the greatest speech was made by the man from New Brunswick. When he talked the reporters forgot their duties, and, instead of taking down the address, listened spellbound. Others threw down their pencils, for they knew that no report they could make would do justice to the power and beauty of that great speech. When the convention was over, Wilmot was called the greatest orator on the continent.

Wilmot's grandfather was one of the Loyalists who had settled on the St. John River, and it was on the banks of that river that Lemuel spent his boyhood. From a child he loved his home, and as he grew older he became interested in the welfare of his countrymen. When he was still a very young man he began to try to bring about reforms in the government of the province.

These reforms had long been needed. You will remember that, when the province was first formed, Sir Guy Carleton's brother Thomas was made governor. Now, in one thing, Thomas Carleton was not like Sir Guy, for he did not think nearly so much about the welfare of the people under his charge. During the last fourteen years that he was governor of the province he lived in England, and left the affairs of New Brunswick pretty much in the hands of his council. This council, which consisted of about twelve members, was much like the Family Compact in Ontario. The members held their offices for life, and were not responsible to the people. They sat with closed doors, so that the people had no way of finding out what was being done. This condition of affairs went on under the governors who followed Carleton, and the members of the Assembly elected by the people had but little power. The council was misusing the money of the country, which should have been spent in building bridges and making roads and improving the province.

As soon as Wilmot entered the House of Assembly he began to take a very active part. He made speech after speech in which he exposed the wrongdoings of the Family Compact, and he used his fine voice and his gift of eloquence to plead for necessary reforms in New Brunswick. Under so able a leader the people became more hopeful of better times.

One of the greatest grievances of the day was the management of the Crown Lands—that is, the lands still owned by the Government. The commissioner who had charge of these lands was paid a ridiculously large salary, and was favoring the members of the Family Compact, some of whom were becoming rich lumbermen, while very little money was left to spend on improving the country. Against this, Wilmot spoke again and again. Finally, he led the Assembly in demanding a statement of what had been done with regard to the Crown Lands during the past year.

Responsible Government

The governor and his council refused to give any statement. Then Mr. Wilmot and another friend of the people went to England to petition the king to grant the right of the members of the Assembly, the men who represented the people, to control the money of the country. At the king's court they were successful; King William the Fourth granted the petition.

Upon hearing this the governor resigned. The new governor appointed in his place was **Sir John Harvey**, who had fought in the war of 1812. He understood the people of New Brunswick better than the governor he followed, and he saw that Wilmot, the great speaker of the Assembly, had the welfare of the province at heart, and that the reforms he proposed were just and wise.

Lemuel Wilmot gave great attention to school matters, and had much to do with bringing about a system of free schools which made it possible for every child, no matter how poor, to have an education. Though he was so great a man, and so busy a man, he never forgot the lonely little children on the far-away clearings. In one of his great speeches he said:

"It is unpardonable that any child should grow up in our country without the benefit of at least a common school education. It is the right of the child. ... I want the children of the poor in the remote settlements to receive the same advantages which are given to the more fortunate children of the towns. ... I know that in many a remote hamlet, amid many a painful scene of poverty and toil, there may be found young minds as ardent and worthy of cultivation as those of any of the pampered children of our cities. It is greatly important to the advancement of the country that these should be instructed."

Wilmot lived to see the people of his province in possession of the rights for which he had struggled. Before his death he filled the position of Lieutenant-governor of New Brunswick.

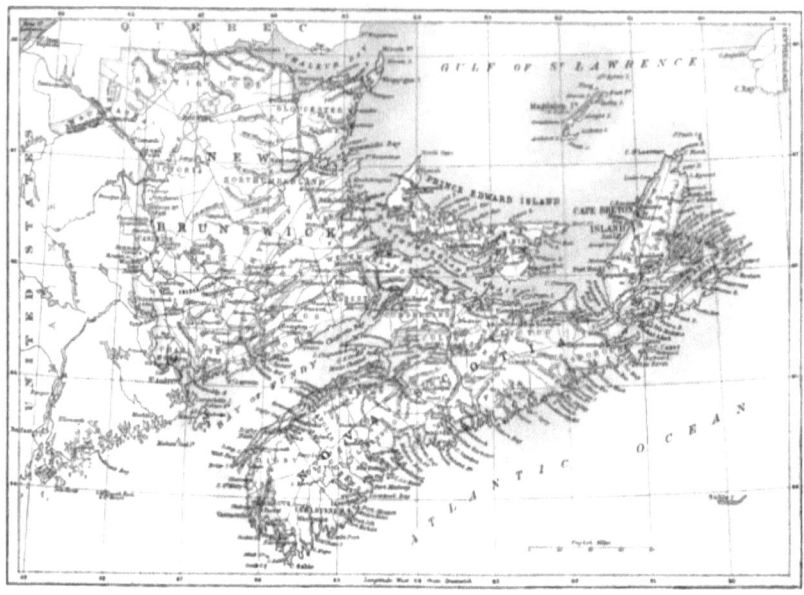

Joseph Howe

In Nova Scotia there were much the same troubles that there were in New Brunswick. The affairs of the country were dealt with by a Family Compact, a council of twelve, which, like the council of New Brunswick, managed the country with closed doors and refused to listen to the wishes of the people.

However, this was not to last always. The Family Compact little guessed that among the boys at school was one who would someday bring about the overthrow of their power. In the summer of 1814 no one would have believed that a little boy of ten years, named **Joseph Howe** (1804-1873), would become one of the greatest men of Nova Scotia. He was not thought to be a very clever boy at school. Often he did not know his lessons, and once he was called a regular little dunce. But few boys made such good comrades, or could lead in the games or manage a boat as he did.

Responsible Government

His home was on the banks of Halifax Harbor, and he would spend hours in the garden watching the sea. He loved nature, and was always happy when out of doors.

But life was not to be all play. At the age of thirteen he began to work in a printing-office. This was the beginning of his education as a newspaper man. A few years later he wrote a poem which so pleased the governor of Nova Scotia that he invited the unknown young poet to visit him at Government House.

By the time Howe was about twenty-four years old he had a newspaper of his own, called the Nova Scotian. And now his real work was to begin. Other papers had not dared to take up the wrongdoings of the Family Compact, but Howe was not afraid to do so. He was a great writer, and through the pages of his paper he fought for the rights of the people of Nova Scotia. This enraged the friends of the Family Compact, and many were watching for an opportunity to bring a lawsuit against the brilliant young editor.

In the year 1835 their chance came. Howe published a very strong article against the doings of the Family Compact, in which the magistrates were accused of defrauding the city of four thousand dollars a year. The Family Compact were indignant. The name of the writer was not given, but they knew that it was Joseph Howe who had published it, and they sent him notice that on a certain day he would be tried for criminal libel. This meant that if he were found guilty he would be imprisoned.

The lawyers to whom he went refused to plead his case. On the day of the trial Howe went into the crowded courtroom with no one to speak for him. But he felt that it was a righteous cause. The freedom of the people to speak their minds was at stake, and though judge, jury, and magistrates were against him he was not afraid.

For six hours he addressed the jury. He spoke with such power that the crowds applauded again and again, and again and again were moved to tears. When it was over the jury declared Joseph Howe not guilty. His friends carried him home in triumph. The crowd followed, and would not go away until their hero had addressed them from a window of his house.

At the time that the rebellion was going on in Upper and Lower Canada, Joseph Howe was the leader of the Reformers in Nova Scotia. For years he worked for responsible government. But he did not work as Mackenzie and Papineau did. Howe did not believe in fighting in that way. He fought only by speaking and writing. Again and again in his most brilliant language he attacked the council for sitting with closed doors, thus keeping from the people what should be public business. When this did not make them open their doors he drew up twelve resolutions condemning the Family Compact, and accusing them of putting their own interests before the public good. After this he was bitterly attacked for days by friends of the council. In reply to these attacks he made another great speech which lasted for eight hours, and ranks among the greatest speeches ever heard in a British Parliament.

By this remarkable speech Joseph Howe made both friends and enemies. The son of the chief justice challenged him to a duel. Howe had no wish to fight, but he could not refuse without being called a coward, so at the early morning hour which had been appointed he went out to meet his opponent. But he made sure he would not kill him, for he let him shoot first, and then fired off his own pistol in the air. He refused all others who would have fought duels with him, saying that his country still needed him, and he had no wish to make a target of himself.

Responsible Government

Later, he wrote a series of letters to the Home Government on the need for responsible government to keep the colonies loyal to the motherland. His work had not been in vain. By the year 1849 he had the satisfaction of seeing responsible government established in Nova Scotia.

The last office which Joseph Howe ever filled was that of Lieutenant-governor of his beloved Nova Scotia. This was only a few weeks before his death. He died at Government House in 1873.

Chapter 12
Progress of the Country

Canada was now a very different place from the Canada of years ago. The settlers had a much easier time than those who came when the country was all forest. Then they all had to work at cutting away the bush. Now some, instead of cutting trees down, were planting them. They were setting out orchards of apples, plums, and cherries, and boys and girls enjoyed picking the ripe fruit.

There were great stretches of large farms where fine crops were raised, and there were towns within reach where they could market their produce.

The wild animals did not like these changes, and made their homes far back in the woods. The Canadians did not object to this, for they were not dependent upon the fur trade as they had been in Champlain's day. They had their crops now, and they could get on with their farming much better without bears and wolves to carry off their sheep, and
skunks, weasels, and foxes to run away with their chickens. Besides their farming, Canadians had their forests, which they were turning into lumber, and their fisheries to bring them in money.

It was easier for the people to trade than it had been years ago, for they had a faster way of getting about and of moving their goods. There were several railways now. The first one to be built was a short line in Lower Canada. The first train was drawn by horses, and was not unlike our old-fashioned street cars.

It was not long, however, before steam engines were used. Some people were afraid of them at first, and declared that they would never ride on anything so fast and noisy. The Indigenous peoples, accustomed to the silent little canoes, thought them deafening. But this was only at first. People soon saw what a fine thing they were for the country. Those who lived away from the waterfront, and had been obliged to cart their goods on heavy wagons drawn by oxen over the rough roads, found the train the greatest convenience. The people of the little far-away villages were especially glad of them, for they could get their mail more regularly than when they had to depend upon the stage-coach, so often delayed by bad roads or stormy weather.

In early days there was no way of taking large boats past the rapids, and all who wanted to go up the St. Lawrence had to go in the Durham boats, which were small flat-bottomed boats that could be dragged over the rapids. Travelling in this way was very slow and often unpleasant, for there was nothing to protect the passengers from wind and rain. One little girl who brought her doll all the way from England, and kept it safe on the ocean, had it quite spoiled on the Durham boats during a rainstorm.

Fortunately for the little girls, their dolls, and all the grown people coming to Canada, canals were built along these rapids. Large boats could sail through the canals, and so pass the rapids. A canal was even built to pass the great Niagara Falls.

Another improvement was the steamboat. The first one in Canada was launched on the St. Lawrence River before the War of 1812. On her first trip she carried only ten passengers, but when she landed she was crowded with visitors. Everyone wanted to see the wonderful boat that wind could not stop. The First Nations peoples stared in amazement, and one old chief said, "The work of the white man, it is great."

Soon larger and stronger steamboats were built, and at Quebec in 1831 the *Royal William* was built. This was the first boat to steam all the way across the ocean; which was a great honor for Canada.

Stamp commemorating the Royal William

A few years later they began to talk of having the mail carried by steamboat. We are told that Joseph Howe from Nova Scotia set out for England in the mail boat when it was still the old-time sailing-vessel. A steamer on her first trip overtook them. There was a dead calm, and as the sailing ship was scarcely moving the steamer passed it and was soon out of sight.

Standing on the deck of the motionless ship, watching the steamer disappear in the distance, and wishing with all his heart that he were on it, Joseph Howe saw plainly the advantage of the steamboat over the sail-boat. In England he did all he could to arrange for a steam mail line, and soon the sail-boat ceased to carry Canada's mail.

In 1847 Canada's first telegraph line was put up. It connected Montreal, Toronto, and Buffalo. It was a great curiosity to the children, who were anxious to find how a message could be sent by what they called "a wire twisted around a bottle every here and there." Many stones were thrown at the bottles by schoolboys, who thought if they could only break one and see what was inside, they might find out the mystery. The telegraph soon became so common that children ceased to wonder.

It was a still greater surprise to the boys and girls when they heard that a cable had been laid between Prince Edward Island and New Brunswick, and that telegrams could now be sent under water. This was the first cable of the New World. It was laid in 1852.

Sixteen years later the great transatlantic cable was laid across the ocean. But a message was no sooner cabled over to Canada than the line broke: a great disappointment after the hard work. Eight years later another was laid and used successfully.

The days had gone when Talon had to put the laws up at the church doors. There were now plenty of papers, and no one need remain ignorant of the affairs of the country.

The Gazette was a favorite name with the early newspaper men. Every province seemed to want a paper of that name. The first paper of Canada was the Halifax Gazette, the second was the Quebec Gazette, and in New Brunswick we read of the Royal Gazette. Even in far-away British Columbia the first paper, though published at a later date, was called the Victoria Gazette.

Magazines were started in Canada, and books were being written by Canadians. Mrs. Moody wrote several books about life in Canada, telling of the funny times the early settlers had when they started housekeeping in the woods. Her stories were true, and so full of excitement that those who read them declared them to be as interesting as a fairy tale.

A man in Nova Scotia wrote a book that made everyone who read it laugh. It was all about Sam Slick, a funny Yankee clock-peddler, who sold his wares in Canada.

Little children had schools to go to now much like the schools in Canada today, only, of course, not such good ones. Some of the schoolhouses in country places were little log buildings with long benches without backs, which must have been very uncomfortable for the pupils. As time went by great improvements were made.

The best schools in those days were in Upper Canada. This was partly because **Egerton Ryerson** (1803–1882), a man greatly interested in education, lived there. He travelled about, visiting the schools of many countries, and returned to tell the Canadians of the best systems of education he had found. Egerton Ryerson is called the father of our public school system.

Part 3
Rupert's Land: The Great West

Chapter 13
The Land Beyond the Great Lakes

No Man's Land

By this time the Europeans had gone to live in the country beyond the Great Lakes which is called the Canadian West. There are many stories of the explorers and settlers who first went into these wilds. But before you read of them, suppose you take a journey through the West in those early days and see the country as the European first found it when he called it "No Man's Land." You cannot take a real one, of course, for the country is very different now, but you can "make believe" and travel in the long ago.

As you follow the canoe route into the country, you will see many streams that have been dammed by beavers to form the ponds where they have built their log houses. They were not so shy in those days as they are now. They cut down the trees and made their homes in parts of the country where today they dare not venture.

Then you come to the level land covered with tall, coarse grass and flowers, stretching away to meet the sky in beautiful curves like the waves of the sea. These are the prairies, the home of the buffalo. If you listen you will hear a rumbling noise, and in the distance you can see a cloud of dust. Hundreds and hundreds of these great animals are galloping over the prairies. They will be far beyond your sight before they stop. This may be only play, for in those days they did not start at every noise, or fear that every sound of crackling leaves or every dark cloud was a prairie fire coming upon them.

Prairie or forest fires did not happen often in the days before the Europeans came, for the First Nations were very careful to stamp out every spark of their campfire before they left the spot. They knew how terrible it would be for the people and the animals living in that part of the country if there should be one spark left to be fanned into flame by the rising wind, and carried on till miles and miles of prairie were one crackling, blazing fire.

Among the other great animals that live in that country is one which the buffaloes do not care to meet. That is the grizzly bear. But they are safe when winter begins, for then the bear will hunt up a cave or hole and go to sleep till he thinks spring has come. Just when this is, is said to depend upon the sun on a certain day. You have heard that every well-conducted bear is supposed to come out of his nest on the second of February. If he cannot see his shadow he stays out; then mild winds blow and spring comes early. But if he sees his shadow he goes back to sleep for six weeks more, while the winds are cold and Jack Frost capers in the air.

A little further on you see tipis. These are the homes of the Plain Cree people, so called because they are the Cree that live on the plains or prairies. If you wish to lodge with them you will not need money, for it would be useless to them, and besides they do not expect pay for what they do for strangers. They will give you a buffalo robe to sit upon and buffalo meat to eat. Then if you can persuade them to talk they will tell you stories of buffalo hunts. They talk first of that huge animal, because on it they depend for clothes, robes, covering for their tipis, strings for their bows, even robes to be wrapped in when they are dead.

"But are you not afraid you will kill them all and have no buffaloes left?" you ask.

"Oh no," they say, "buffaloes keep coming," and they point away towards the distance.

"What do you mean?" you ask.

Then the old man begins to talk. He says that far away is a lake whose waters are never still because from under the lake comes the buffalo. On the shores are always heard sounds of buffaloes fighting, ever fighting to be the first out on the prairies. So they believe there will always be buffaloes because the lake from which they come will always be there.

Buffalo Hunt by George Catlin (1844)

Now you travel through the land of the Wood Cree and the Chipewyan people. With a few blue beads and an awl you can persuade a young brave from almost any tepee to guide you. Though the guide may take you to the homes of tribes who do not speak as he does, he can make them understand him, for the First Nations have a sign language which they all know. Before you go far you will see a flock of deer swimming across a stream. Some have reached the opposite bank. How beautiful they look! Among the trees, feeding on the tender branches, is a moose, an animal that is not at all pretty. He has a long head, somewhat like that of a horse, and a crooked nose that is very ugly. His big ears must be sharp, for he has heard you already. How awkwardly he runs, but he knows how to get over the ground, even though he is going among the trees and has great horns. Your guide tells you that he will not stop until he is far away, but that when the deer run from you they go only a little way, and then stop and look to see if there is any danger.

While you have been busy watching the animals, the guide has been hanging a piece of birch bark on a stake.

"Why are you doing this, and what are those drawings you have made on it?" you ask.

"It is to show all the people who pass that this is a good hunting-ground," he explains. "This mark shows that there are many deer and moose here."

"But deer and moose do not stay in the same place. Some months from now the hunter who sees this may waste his days here and find nothing," you reply.

The wise man has made no mistake. He points to other drawings on his birch bark. To the First Nations a month is a moon, and to each moon they have given a name. This guide's tribe call March the Eagle moon; April the Goose moon; May, Frog moon; June, the moon in which the birds begin to lay their eggs; July, the moon when the birds begin to cast their feathers; August, the moon when the young birds begin to fly; and September, the moon when the leaves fall.

There on his birch bark is the bird which gives the name to the present moon or month, and there is the moon almost full as

Land Beyond the Great Lakes

it is now. From these drawings a hunter will know what month the deer and moose were seen here, and what time in the month.

As you travel on you see dried meat and fine furs beside a big crooked tree. Ask your guide why they have been left there, and he will tell you that his people have placed them there as an offering to the Great Spirit, Manitou.

"Are they not afraid that some cold, hungry person will take them away?"

"No person would do that for fear of making the Great Spirit angry," the guide replies.

How lonely it is travelling through this great country! It seems too large even for the thousands of animals and First Nations. But they want plenty of room. To live in the midst of a wilderness is their delight. What frightens us is a joy to them. They never lose their way.

By-and-by you reach a river and travel by canoe. You need not fear the rapids and sharp rocks when an Indigenous person paddles. He can guide the canoe safely past all dangers. After a time you leave the canoe and go through the woods. How quickly your guide walks, and how his sharp eyes peer everywhere! You wonder how he knows which way to go in these dense woods.

That night you go to sleep with the blue sky for a roof and the stars for candles. In the morning you are off again. By noonday you see a group of moose-skin tepees, the homes of the Wood Cree. They spread a beautiful bearskin for you to sit upon, and bring you rabbit soup and moose meat.

Outside the puppy dogs are playing with sticks, and the fat little papooses are pinching them and pulling their ears. There is a funny little boy holding one end of a piece of dried meat in his mouth and trying to saw off the other end with a sharp stone. Up in a tree, safe from the dogs, they keep the meat. Slices of it are hanging over the fire to dry. You see a queer-looking thing hanging in the tree in front of one of the tipis. It is a First Nations medicine bag, and on no account must you touch it. It is so sacred to the person who owns it that he will not even talk about it, and you can never persuade him to tell you what he has in it.

As you travel on you see many foxes, rabbits, and pretty white ermines with their black-tipped tails. Certainly, the wild creatures wear rich, handsome clothing. One day, when far in the north, you hear a shrill scream. Your guide tells you that it is made by a bird called the alarm bird, because it has a habit of flying back and forth from one group of moving objects to another, uttering a peculiar scream, and in that way often warns Indigenous peoples of approaching enemies. This alarm bird is warning you that you are nearing the Inuit, the people that live on the Arctic coast, farther north than any other race in the world.

Soon you see little huts covered with skins and shaped something like a tipi. These are the summer homes of the Inuit. The Inuit come out to meet you. What beautiful bright brown eyes they have! To see as far as they do you would have to look through a telescope. The Inuit all have rich fur clothing. Each baby is carried on its mother's back in a hood or pocket of her dress until old enough to have a fur coat of its own. One of the Inuit is coming in with a seal, and they are going to have a feast. They will eat it raw, and drink the blood out of little sealskin cups. No wonder they were once called "Eskimos", a name which means eaters of raw flesh.

As you do not care to join the feast, you might like to walk along the shore. There is a man coming in an Inuit canoe or kayak. How fast he makes it go with that double-bladed paddle. The canoe is not made of birch bark: there are no birch trees growing here. It is covered with seal-skin, off which the hair has been scraped. The oily skin has been stretched over a frame and joined with double seams, so that it will not leak. Unlike the canoes of the First Nations, the top is covered, leaving a round hole in the middle, so that when the Inuit gets in, only the top part of his body is seen, and his feet will never be wet with the spray. But to keep dry is not the reason that the top is covered. If you watch a little longer you will see his kayak tip against a piece of floating ice and upset. If he were in a First Nation canoe he would save himself by holding to the bottom of it. But up he comes, sitting in the canoe just as he was before. He had tied his waterproof skin coat so tightly about the rim of the round opening that the water could not rush in. In that kind of canoe he is like a rubber ball, and just as safe. If the playful walrus, which swims in that sea, should come along and upset his boat, it will be fun for walrus and Inuit alike.

When you walk down the shore out of sight of the Inuit, you see a white bear swimming with her cubs. Many of the animals that live in the land of the Inuit, where there is snow and ice nearly all the year, are white; but the little rabbit has such bright black eyes that he must be sure to close them if he wants to curl up and be taken for a snowball. The seals, which are not white, often have a hard time trying to keep out of the way when Inuit and polar bears want them for their supper.

As the days go by a great change takes place in the Inuit land. There was no night when you first went there, but now the nights have grown long, and snow and ice have come. The Inuit have moved into their round-topped snow-houses. They think them very cozy homes.

They have plenty of warm furs for beds, clear pieces of ice for windows, and a lamp which they make by carving a half-moon shaped vessel out of soft stone, filling it up with seal oil, and putting in a wick. It is very dreary here in the winter, for the sun will not rise for many weeks. The winter is like one long, long night. It will be made up to the Inuit, however, when they have their summer, and the sun shines at midnight. But it is not a pleasant time for you to visit there, so while King Winter reigns in the north you would do better to travel south and cross over to the Pacific coast.

On the way you see a great herd of reindeer, enough to make hundreds of teams for Santa Claus. How pretty they are! Farther on you see a moose-skin tepee, and you stop there to see what the people are doing in this dull weather. You find that, though it is quite early in the afternoon, the children who have been playing in the snow are going in because it is getting dark. The women are sitting by the fire making rabbit-skin clothing for the little ones. The men are playing some kind of game which the children begin to play too. If you watch the game you will see that one shakes sticks about in his hands, and another guesses which hand they are in, a forfeit being paid when the guess is right. They are so interested in their game that they play nearly all night.

Land Beyond the Great Lakes

Photograph of Inuit children in 1925

Before you cross the mountains, you will go to see some of the Blackfoot tribe. These tribes live just east of the Rockies. You find them painting their faces, getting out their war-caps, and preparing for their war-dance and war-feast.

After crossing the mountains, you find a First Nation of people that have oddly shaped heads. When they are children boards are fastened on their heads to make them grow in the flat shape which these people admire. You come to another tribe, called the Tacullies, which, in their own language, means people who go upon the water. They take this name because they go from one village to another in canoes.

These Tacullies, or Carriers, are a talkative people, and when not talking they want to be always humming or whistling, or making some noise. When a number of them are in a hut together it is like a school at recess time.

Along the coast many people have robes of very handsome fur. Out in the water you see the beautiful sea-otters from which they get them. Some are swimming, and you see them every now and then stretching up their pretty heads to look about. Some are resting on the seaweed or sitting on the rocks smoothing their hair as cats do. Others are on their backs in the water, holding the baby sea-otters in their arms much as people hold their children, for the little ones cannot swim until they are several months old. No otter can live long under the water, so in times of storm when the ocean is rough they must come to the shore. In early days these beautiful creatures were very numerous along that coast, but when the fur traders came they were killed for their fur in such numbers that almost none are left.

Explorers of the West

Henry Hudson

For a long time, as you know, the Europeans believed that the continent of America was only a narrow strip of land with a sea beyond, across which they could sail to Asia. For many years they tried to find a water passage through the new continent to the sea, so that they would have a water route all the way to India and China. In trying to find a way to the riches of the East, they discovered the wealth of the West.

In Champlain's day a man named **Henry Hudson** (1565-1611) sailed across the Atlantic in a boat called the Half Moon to search for a water passage to the Western Sea. He sailed into bays and inlets along the coast, but found no passage through the land.

After this he determined to search the coast-line farther north. So he crossed the ocean again in a new boat called the Discovery. Then he sailed north until he came to Hudson Bay. Thinking there might be a water passage opening out of it, he remained on its shores until the ice was gone in the spring and he could sail across the bay and see what was beyond. His men had been very weary of the long cold winter, and when spring came they wanted to return without searching for the north-west passage. Because Henry Hudson would not consent to this they put him adrift in an open boat, with his son and a few of the men who were ill, and then sailed home, leaving them to perish on those wild northern waters. Our great bay in the north is named after poor Henry Hudson, whose grave is somewhere under its waves.

Henry Hudson

Arrival of Radisson in an Indigenous Camp, by C.W. Jeffreys (1869-1951)

Radisson and Groseilliers

When men heard of the great northern bay which Hudson had found by sailing north along the coast, they began to wonder whether it could be reached by going overland. Two men who thought much about this were **Pierre Radisson** (1636-1710) and his brother-in-law **Médard des Groseilliers** (1618-1696). About this time some Indigenous fur traders came down the Ottawa to Three Rivers, where these men lived. While there they told Groseilliers that far away to the north, in the country past the Great Lakes, was a large body of salt water. Groseilliers felt sure that this was Hudson Bay, and told Radisson about it. After talking it over they determined to set out together to explore that country and learn for themselves what was to be found there. A party of

Algonquins who lived far away in that direction, and were now returning after trading their furs to the French, promised to guide them back.

Beyond the straits of Mackinaw the explorers turned northward. It was winter by that time, and they travelled on snowshoes. At last they met with Indigenous people who described a great bay in the north, the water of which was "bitter to drink," and they told the Frenchmen how to reach it. It was the bay that Hudson had found. By this journey Radisson and Groseilliers had learned that it could be reached from Canada by land. Whether they themselves reached its shores is not known.

After returning home the explorers set out upon another long journey. This time they had to steal away in the night. It seems that the governor would not give them the right to trade in the furs of the country they were going to explore unless they would promise to give him half the profits. This they refused to do. Then he forbade them to leave Three Rivers. They stole away in the dark, but their guides had not waited for them, and to overtake them Radisson and Groseilliers had to travel day and night.

On this journey they travelled north-west from Lake Superior until they came to the villages of the Cree people. They were the first Europeans the Cree had ever seen. They gave them a grand feast, and showed them that they would be their friends and help them always. By giving these people brass awls, needles, or rings for their furs, Radisson and Groseilliers made the first beginning in the fur trade of the Canadian West.

Verendrye
One of the greatest explorers of the Canadian West was a Frenchman named **Pierre Verendrye** (1685-1749). At one time he was in charge of a fur-trading post on Lake Nipigon. To this post came

First Nations people who had travelled far and knew much about the country. They told Verendrye of the land beyond the Great Lakes, and drew maps on birch bark showing the country they had gone through. One old chief, who seemed to have travelled further than the others, said he had gone down a river and had come to water which ebbed and flowed, and that he had met with people who told him that beyond that river was salt water. Now Verendrye thought that the water which ebbed and flowed must be the tide, and that the salt water beyond must be the Western Sea, and he said he would go to find it. Then he went down to Montreal to see if the governor would help him. The governor gave him permission to trade in furs in the country he was going to explore, and then the merchants readily consented to give him the supplies he needed and take their payment in furs when his canoes came back.

He set out with his three sons and his nephew, his voyageurs, and an interpreter. Travelling by canoe was slow and difficult, and it was autumn by the time they reached the most distant fur post. Late as it was, some of the party went on through the unexplored country and built a fort on Rainy Lake in which to spend the winter. Some time after this they reached Lake Winnipeg, and built a fort there where they could trade with the First Nations. These first forts were only tiny buildings made of rough logs.

Many disasters befell the lonely travelers. One of the saddest of these was the death of Verendrye's nephew while travelling from one fort to another. But the most terrible of all was that known as the Lake of the Woods tragedy. This happened when Verendrye's eldest son, Father Aulneau, the priest who was with them, and some of the men were returning to Fort Michilimackinac for supplies. It seems that some Cree who had just traded their furs for guns had fired at some Sioux, and then shouted to them that they were Frenchmen. The Sioux believed this, and were very angry. They said they had never injured the French, and they would pay them back for firing upon them for no reason. So when they saw this little party of Frenchmen camped on an island they came up stealthily and killed them all.

This was a great grief to poor Verendrye. But though he was sad and discouraged, he travelled on. There were many other things to discourage him. Jealous traders in Montreal said that he was only working for his own interests. Because of this the merchants sometimes refused to send him the goods he needed unless he first sent them furs. But in spite of all this, he still hoped to find the Western Sea. The First Nations he met with were kind to him. They called him "Father," and helped him in many ways.

Another fort was built on a spot which is now part of Winnipeg, and one where Portage la Prairie is now. One of his sons reached the spot where the north and south Saskatchewan rivers meet, and also travelled as far as the Rocky Mountains. He would have climbed the mountains and searched beyond them for the Western Sea, but his guides would go no farther, so he had to turn back.

Verendrye died in Montreal while preparing to set out upon another journey in search of the Western Sea. He had explored much of the country, smoked the peace pipe with many different tribes of First Nations, and opened up a great fur trade; but he had not made his way across the continent. Men had not yet learned how broad a land it is.

Samuel Hearne
It was **Samuel Hearne** (1745-1792) who first went overland to the Arctic Ocean from a trading post on the shores of Hudson Bay. On his way he had to pass through that cold, bleak part of

the country which even the animals avoid, and which men call the "Barren Lands." For days at a time he went without food, and slept night after night in the snow. After travelling for months he came to the Coppermine River, and saw where it flows into the Arctic Ocean. Near the mouth of the river he saw the homes of the Inuit. After this his guides led him to the copper mines, where they got the metal for knives and hatchets. Samuel Hearne was the first European man to reach the shores of the Arctic Ocean; but he, too, failed to discover a north-west passage.

Alexander Mackenzie

After this another explorer made two great journeys. **Alexander Mackenzie** (1764–1820) was his name. He started from a trading post on Lake Athabasca, which you can find on your maps. He set out from there with four birch-bark canoes and travelled north to Great Slave Lake. He discovered the Mackenzie River, which was afterwards named after him, and traced it to its mouth. On his way he met with many different tribes of First Nations. At almost every camp he could get someone to go with them as guide until they reached the next encampment, where they could get another guide. At the coast he saw the homes of the Inuit; but the Inuit themselves were away hunting whales, his Indigenous guides said.

Land Beyond the Great Lakes

Alexander Mackenzie

After this he made his way across the country to the Pacific Ocean by following the Peace River through the Rocky Mountains. He was the first European man to reach the Pacific Coast by land. The journey was full of terrible hardships, and often he and his men were hungry and discouraged. Many a time their lives were in danger, especially when going through the mountains. In some places the river was full of angry rapids and huge rocks, while on each side towered the great hills. Pieces of rock from their steep sides fell around the travelers.

Where the river was impassable they were obliged to drag the canoe by means of a line, which was often broken on the sharp boulders. At one place, where there was no room between the deep water and the mountain, they had to climb a steep hillside, cutting their way through the trees, and carrying the canoe and all the baggage. Their moccasins were soon in holes, and their feet grew sore.

It was lonely, too, travelling over the unknown land, and he must have felt very much as Columbus did when making his first voyage. But of course Mackenzie often met with First Nations, and by making signs could sometimes learn from them what was before him. Then, too, he had his Indigenous guides. What would the explorers have done without the help of the First Nations?

Upon reaching the coast he took some vermilion, such as the First Nations used, mixed it with grease, and on the cliff overhanging the ocean, wrote: "Alexander Mackenzie, from Canada by land, the twenty-second of July, one thousand seven hundred and ninety-three."

Although the winter's frost and summer's heat of over one hundred years have wiped out the mark upon this rock, his name still lives in the Great Mackenzie River.

Captain Cook

European men had already reached the western coast of what is now British Columbia. But they had not gone from Canada by land. They had sailed round the Cape of Good Hope in the south of Africa, and across the Indian and Pacific Oceans.

About the time that Verendrye was listening to the old chief's story of saltwater far to the west, a boy in England was listening to stories of a wonderful shore, where sea-otters lived in crowds and huge mountains towered up to the clouds. This boy, whose name was James Cook, became a great sailor, and was sent out by England to search along the north-west coast of America for a water passage through the continent.

Upon reaching the Pacific Coast he anchored at a bay which, as he afterwards learned, was called Nootka. It is now known as Nootka Sound. The Indigenous people were not at all afraid of the strangers in their big boat. They decorated their hair with feathers, got into their finest canoes, and went out singing to meet them, and their chief made a long speech of welcome. Cook landed near the homes of these people, and traded with them while he repaired his ship. They brought him the skins of the beaver and the beautiful sea-otter. What they seemed to like best in return for these were brass buttons off the sailors' coats and rusty nails from the ship.

After leaving this friendly tribe Cook sailed north along the coast, searching for the water passage through the land. He saw the crowds of sea-otters, the herds of walrus, and the great mountains he had heard of when a boy; but he found no north-west passage. He sailed as far as Behring Strait; then, being sure that there was no water passage through the land, he started back. This was fifteen years before Mackenzie reached the Pacific Coast.

Indigenous wolf mask from Nootka Sound, allegedly recovered by James Cook and his crew in 1778

Vancouver

Cook's report that there was no water passage through America was not believed in England. Some years after his voyage, when they heard that the Spaniards were taking possession of Nootka, they sent **Captain George Vancouver** (1757–1798) to America to claim that coast by right of Cook's discovery. He was also to search for the Northwest Passage.

Vancouver explored Juan de Fuca Strait, and gave his own name to the great island which has ever since been known as Vancouver Island. After that he explored the west coast of Canada so thoroughly, that men were at last convinced that there was no water passage through the continent.

Map of Vancouver Island

Chapter 14
The Fur-Traders and the First Colony

The Fur-Traders

Had you travelled through the northwest in the days of these early explorers, you would have found here and there in that great country little log buildings, each with a red flag floating over it. On the flags were the letters "H.B.C." These letters stood for "Hudson's Bay Company," the name of the great fur-trading company which has been in existence since the days of Radisson and Groseilliers. You remember that these explorers were the first men to trade with the Indigenous people of the Canadian West. They were also the men who brought about the forming of the Hudson's Bay Company.

A station of the Hudson's Bay Company

It happened in this way. When they returned from the northwest, the governor took most of the furs they brought back as a fine, imposed because they had gone without his permission. He also refused to give them the right to go back again and trade with the First Nations. Without the profits from the fur trade Radisson and Groseilliers could not afford to explore the country as they wished to do. In despair they went to France, hoping that the king would help them. But the king was too busy to think about the explorers, so they went to England to see if anyone there would listen to them. In England **Prince Rupert** (1619-1682), the king's cousin, took a great interest in what they told him of the riches to be gained from the fur trade in the New World. He induced a company of merchants to fit out two ships and send them to Hudson Bay to bring back some of those beautiful skins the explorers were talking about.

Radisson sailed in one of these ships and Groseilliers in the other. The ship in which Radisson sailed was driven back by storms, but the one in which Groseilliers sailed reached Hudson Bay, and came safely back loaded with rich furs.

When the merchants saw these the Hudson's Bay Company was formed. To this company the king gave the sole right to the fur trade in that "great lone land," and the right to rule over the country. Prince Rupert was made governor of the company, and the land under their rule was called Rupert's Land.

The Hudson's Bay Company sent men out to trade with the First Nations, and soon forts were built at different places through the country where the Indigenous hunters could bring their furs.

That is the reason why there was a fort on the shores of Hudson Bay, from which Samuel Hearne set out upon his journey to

The Fur-Traders and the First Colony

the Arctic Ocean, and that is the reason why the animals were growing wilder than they had been before.

The First Nations now had another purpose in hunting than that of supplying themselves with food and clothing. Besides, they were hunting now with guns and steel traps, which were far more dangerous to the animals than anything they had ever had in their land before. It seemed as if they were forgetting that they had called the wild creatures their younger brothers.

In the early spring, just before the snow became too soft for travelling, the First Nations would take their sleigh loads of furs down to the nearest forts. If it happened that they could go by river, they would wait until the ice had broken up and take their canoes.

Had you visited one of these lonely forts in the winter, you would have found solitary Canadian men, with nothing to do but keep their fires going and write letters for the next post, which might not be for many months. But if you had gone in the early springtime, when the First Nations were coming in with furs, you would find them very, very busy. For then they must smoke the peace pipe, count the furs they brought, and give them their value in the goods they chose from the storeroom.

The First Nations would get their powder and shot first to make sure of being able to hunt the next season. Then they would get some tobacco, a little flour, and perhaps some tea and sugar, which was a great treat to them. If the season had been a good one, they might be able to get a bright-colored cotton handkerchief or a piece of figured calico to delight their wives.

The trader never reckoned the value of furs in money, which was meaningless to the First Nations. Instead, he told the hunter how many beaver skins' worth of goods he might have for his pile of furs.

The Hudson's Bay Company set a good example in their dealings with the First Nations. It was one of their rules that they should be treated kindly. They were always honorable with them, and would not allow them to be cheated in any way. Those who had been unsuccessful in the hunt and had no furs to trade were paid in advance if they were in need. The result was that the First Nations learned to respect the European men and the British flag. The Hudson's Bay Company had no trouble with them, but found them willing to keep their promises and always ready to return a kindness.

This great fur-trading company was not without a rival. After Verendrye explored the country beyond the Great Lakes, many traders from Canada followed in the route he had taken. Before long they found that they must form a company and work together if they were going to keep their share of the fur trade, for the Hudson's Bay Company were building forts nearer and nearer their trading-places and inducing the First Nations to go to them. So in the year 1784 the North-West Company was formed. It was composed chiefly of Montreal merchants. Most of the members were English or Scottish, but usually it was the French voyageurs who took the furs down to the St. Lawrence. For years the North-West Company and the Hudson's Bay Company were rivals in the fur trade. This rivalry ended in 1821, when the North-West Company united with the Hudson's Bay Company.

Lord Selkirk and His Colony
As time went by **Lord Selkirk** (1771–1820), a Scottish nobleman, began to think that the country west of the Great Lakes need no longer be No Man's Land. He said crops could grow and farmers

could live in that land, where until then only the fur traders and the explorers had ventured.

Statue of Lord Selkirk outside the Manitoba Legislative Building

In his own country he had seen many poor men whose farms were so small that they could not raise enough for their families, and many others who had no farms at all. In the new country there was land enough for all. He made up his mind that he would bring some of those poor men out to start a settlement or colony where the Red and Assiniboine Rivers join.

Some men in those days laughed at his plans. They thought it was too cold on the Red River for any colony to live. They had no idea that by-and-by that same spot would be one of the greatest wheat-growing districts in the world. It was years before they believed that Lord Selkirk's little settlement could prosper.

But Lord Selkirk paid no attention to what they said. He believed that he could start a colony on the Red River, and so he began to carry out his plans.

Now this country, as you know, was part of Rupert's Land, and so belonged to the Hudson's Bay Company. As it happened, they were willing that Lord Selkirk should start a settlement there, and sold one hundred thousand square miles of land to him for that purpose. That same year (1811) the first settlers were brought out from Scotland and Ireland. They were taken by way of Hudson's Bay. As they arrived there too late in the season to go overland to Red River that year, they were obliged to spend their first winter in the new world on the shores of Hudson's Bay, finding shelter in the Hudson's Bay Company fort until houses could be put up for them.

In the spring, when the rivers were clear of ice, they set out. They travelled up the river in flat-bottomed boats, crossed Lake Winnipeg, and at last reached their new home in safety.

Now it happened that the North-West Company were determined there should be no colony at Red River. They said the settlers would drive the wild animals further back, so that they would have to move their trading posts. They said, moreover, that the Hudson's Bay Company had no right to sell the land to Lord Selkirk, and that it was not theirs to sell, but belonged to the North-West Company because their traders had been there first. When they heard the settlers were actually coming they declared they would drive them away.

No sooner had the tired colonists reached the Red River than a band of Indigenous peoples, who had been hired by the North-West Company, appeared and ordered them to leave. These were the Métis people, who were descended from both First Nations and French ancestors. They were in war-paint and feathers. The

The Fur-Traders and the First Colony

settlers were much frightened, and, as they could not resist such a force, they allowed themselves to be taken to Pembina, a Hudson's Bay Company post seventy miles away. And there the colonists were obliged to spend the winter.

In the spring (1813) they went back and began to put in their first crops. Fortunately, there were no forests to be cleared away, such as the United Empire Loyalists had to contend with when they settled in Eastern Canada. The next year they were again driven away by the North-West Company. But, undismayed, they returned the following spring, and more settlers arrived.

In the summer of 1816 the "Nor'-Westers," as they were sometimes called, again tried to break up the colony in the same way. When the settlers saw the painted Métis approaching on horseback with tomahawks they were greatly alarmed.

Now at this time Governor Semple was at the Hudson's Bay Company post at Red River. When he saw these armed men coming he took twenty of his men and went to find out their purpose. A fight took place, in which the governor and some of his men were killed, and the others were taken prisoners. This is known as the battle of Seven Oaks. Afterwards the Métis drove the settlers away and burned their houses.

The people were terribly discouraged after this, and felt that to try to build new homes again was almost hopeless. But, fortunately for them, Lord Selkirk had heard of their troubles, and was on his way to them. As soon as he arrived he brought them back to their farms, encouraged them to begin over again, and helped them in many ways. He also had a meeting with the First Nations who lived in the country he had bought from the Hudson's Bay Company. Because they had the first right to it, he made a treaty with them, by which he promised to give them one hundred pounds of tobacco each year in return for their allowing the colonists to have the land. The First Nations consented to this. They were greatly pleased with Lord Selkirk, whom they called the "Silver Chief."

The trials of the Selkirk settlers were not yet at an end. Scarcely had they made a new beginning before another enemy came to them. Their crops were looking well that summer, and their hopes were high for the success of the colony. But one afternoon in July they noticed that it was becoming uncommonly dark. They feared a bad storm was coming up, but it was much worse than that. In a few minutes the air was thick with grasshoppers, which alighted on the ground, covering the land as far as the settlers could see. By next day the crops, the grass, even the leaves on the bushes were eaten. Every green thing was gone.

Once more the heart-broken settlers set out for Pembina. They spent the winter there, and also the following one, for the next summer the young grasshoppers sprang up more numerous than those of the year before. Lord Selkirk, at great expense, bought them seed wheat, and again they made a fresh start.

In 1820 Lord Selkirk died. The next year the North-West Company united with the Hudson's Bay Company, and no longer troubled the colony. Soon after this great company bought back the land Lord Selkirk had purchased.

There was one more disaster. About eight years after the grasshoppers had eaten the crops, the Red River flooded the settlement in the springtime and washed away the houses and barns. The poor people rushed to the high ground for safety, and from there watched their possessions being carried down to Lake Winnipeg. Once more they were obliged to make a new beginning, and before long were able to enjoy the hard-earned days of prosperity.

The Fur-Traders and the First Colony

Twenty-six years later the Red River again flooded its banks. Houses and barns floated off much as they had done before. The water rose with such rapidity that cattle and horses were drowned, and the now homeless people were obliged to take refuge in boats.

This was the last great misfortune which befell the Selkirk settlers, the pioneers of what is now the Province of Manitoba.

Métis camp on Manitoba prairie

A Métis woman in 1886

Chapter 15
Some Great Men and What They Did

Simon Fraser

One of these great men was **Simon Fraser** (1776–1862). Before the North-West Company united with the Hudson's Bay Company he was one of the most enterprising traders among the "Nor'-Westers." After Alexander Mackenzie crossed the Rocky Mountains and found that there was a wide country between the mountains and the sea, Simon Fraser went into that country and built a trading post, and made a beginning in the fur trade in what is now British Columbia. Other trading posts were soon erected, and other traders followed him across the mountains.

But making a beginning in the fur trade in British Columbia was not Fraser's greatest work. He was soon to become a famous explorer. About this time the members of the North-West Company had heard that men from the United States had found the mouth of a large river which was called the Columbia. They knew that when Alexander Mackenzie was making his journey to the sea, he had come to a great river so full of rocks and rapids that he had chosen to walk across the country, rather than to attempt canoeing down so treacherous a stream. Now some believed that this river he had come to was the Columbia, and that in spite of the rocks and rapids it might make a canoe route to and from the coast. So they sent Simon Fraser to follow the river to the sea and find out all about it.

Fraser had a terrible time going down that river. Often the task seemed impossible, but he would not give up. Sometimes he and his men passed the whirlpools by climbing the almost perpendicular banks of rock that rose on either side. When this was impossible they had to risk the dangers of passing the foaming rapids in their frail canoes. More than once a canoe was dashed against the rocks, and the men saved themselves by clinging to the rocks till ropes could be thrown to them from those on shore. Near the coast the waters were calmer, but other troubles came to them. The Indigenous people there were unfriendly. Foreign traders had come to their coast who had not given them a very good impression of the outsiders, and they wanted to drive away all encroaching men who came to their country. But Fraser surmounted all obstacles and reached the mouth of the river.

He found, however, that it was not the Columbia, but a great river which emptied into the Pacific some distance north of the Columbia. Because Fraser followed the river to the sea, it was named after him. Ever since it has been known as the Fraser River.

David Thompson
Three years after Simon Fraser followed that treacherous river to the sea, and found that it was not the Columbia, another explorer reached the mouth of the Columbia River.

This explorer was **David Thompson** (1770–1857), the great geographer and map-maker of the West. Sometime before this, when travelling through the country, he had reached a spot just beyond the summit of the Rocky Mountains, and there had come upon a river of which he had never heard. As he gazed at it he said, "May God in His mercy give me to see where it flows into the ocean and return in safety." Now this river happened to be the upper waters of a tributary of the Columbia. By the summer of 1811 Thompson had reached the mouth of the Columbia, and so had seen where those waters "flowed into the ocean."

Some Great Men

David Thompson came to Canada when a boy of fourteen. His first years in the new country were spent at a Hudson's Bay Company post on the shores of Hudson Bay. Later he went to a trading post on the Saskatchewan River. As he travelled about the country he began to survey the land, and to take notes of all he learned and to draw maps. His notes and maps were so exact that other travelers learned from them into just what sort of country they were going. They knew where they would find great rivers, and where they would find hills or plains, and whether they would have to travel by horseback or canoe.

David Thompson

By the time David Thompson reached the mouth of the Columbia, he could truly write, "Thus I have fully completed the survey of this part of America from sea to sea...and have determined the positions of the mountains, lakes, and rivers, and other remarkable places on the northern part of this continent. The maps of all these surveys have been drawn, and they are laid down in geographical position. This work has occupied me for twenty-seven years."

The Story of Canada

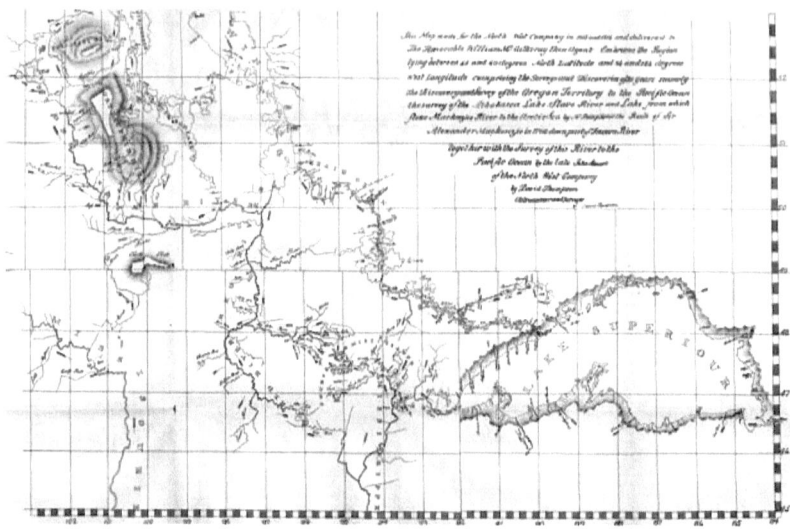

David Thompson's famous map of Western British North America

Sir John Franklin

A little over fifty years after Mackenzie reached the western sea by land, **Sir John Franklin** (1786–1847) tried to find a north-west passage by water. On his first journey he travelled overland through America to the Arctic Ocean, and explored much of the coast, which until then was but little known. After this he set out with two vessels, crossed the Atlantic, sailed north to the Arctic Ocean, and made his way along the Arctic coast, searching for a water passage through to the western sea. Time passed, but he did not return. In England much anxiety was felt, and men set out to search for some trace of his ships. On an island in the Arctic Ocean they found three lonely graves, and so they knew that the ships had sheltered there. Later they found upon the ice a bottle, in which was a paper. On this paper was written a notice of Sir John Franklin's death. All now knew what had been the fate of the brave explorer. From the stories told by the Inuit, and from skeletons which were found, the searchers felt sure that the ships had been caught in the ice, and that after Franklin's death the men in despair had abandoned the boats and tried to travel southward, but had died upon the way. From the explorations of Sir John Franklin it was learned that the Arctic Ocean was blocked by ice, and could never be a north-west passage for trading vessels.

The Search for Sir John Franklin in the Arctic by François Musin (1850)

Sir George Simpson

Sir George Simpson (1792-1860) was one of the greatest governors which the Hudson's Bay Company ever had. He was chosen as governor just after the North-West Company united with the Hudson's Bay Company. This was a time when a strong man was needed. He filled the position so well that he remained governor for thirty-nine years.

Each year he travelled through the country visiting the different trading posts. As he neared a trading post his bugle would sound, a gun would be fired, and then the bagpipes would start some well-known march as his party approached. Sometimes he had meetings among the First Nations, and smoked the peace pipe with them and made speeches to them. In these speeches he never failed to give them plenty of good advice, and to tell them to be sure to bring their furs to his trading posts.

It is little wonder the First Nations thought him a most remarkable man, and were willing to bring their furs to the traders who had such a great man for their chief.

During Sir George Simpson's governorship new trading posts were established, and many more canoe-loads of furs were shipped away than before. The Hudson's Bay Company trade was also extended west of the Rocky Mountains, and their trading posts were built in what is now British Columbia. At that time foreign traders were crossing the sea to that coast, and United States traders were coming from the south. By pushing the Hudson's Bay Company trade to the ocean, and building trading posts there, Sir George Simpson did much towards holding that coast for the British flag.

Paul Kane

Besides the explorers and fur traders, there was an artist who travelled through the West in those early days and painted pictures of the First Nations and their tipis. This artist was **Paul Kane** (1810-1871), a young man who had spent much of his boyhood in sketching the First Nations in Ontario. Later he showed his sketches to Sir George Simpson, and told him of his desire to

Some Great Men

travel through the West and make some paintings of the First Nations, showing them as they lived in those early days before the Europeans had taken their country.

Sir George Simpson was so much interested in the artist and his work that he invited him to go to the West with him in his fleet of canoes. Delighted at this opportunity, Paul Kane set out with the governor. He spent over two years sketching in that country. Sometimes he found it very hard to induce people to pose for him. This was because the First Nations called a portrait of a person his "second self." Now according to an old belief among them, each had a "second self" which carried his messages up to the Great Spirit. And so they feared that if the painter put that "second self" upon his canvas and carried it away, they would be quite out of touch with the Great Spirit, and would have no way of asking for His protection and care. But Paul Kane was able to persuade some of them that if they would let him paint their portraits, the Great Spirit would still watch over them, and no evil would befall them.

In spite of these challenges, and the difficulties of travelling through the country, Paul Kane succeeded in taking home a large collection of paintings. These are very valuable now, for they show how the country used to appear, and how the First Nations used to live.[1]

---

[1] Works from Paul Kane are featured in this book, including the cover image.

Assiniboine Hunting Buffalo by Paul Kane

The Surveyor by Paul Kane

Chapter 16
The Father of British Columbia

James Douglas
You have all heard of the "Black Douglas" of Scottish history. Now, as you know, many Scotsmen were among the men who did great things in the New World in early days. You will not be surprised to learn that a descendant of the Black Douglas did so much for that part of British America which lies west of the Rocky Mountains that he came to be called the Father of British Columbia.

James Douglas (1803-1877) first came to Canada when a boy of seventeen. Though he was so young he was tall, and appeared more like a man than a boy, and some who talked with him said that he had "ideas beyond his age." Having come out to seek his fortunes with the North-West Company, he went directly to Fort William, their headquarters. Now it happened that the very next year (1821) that company united with the Hudson's Bay Company. James Douglas was about to return home to Scotland when something happened which caused him to change his mind. During his short stay at Fort William he had won the friendship of John McLoughlin, the man who was now given charge under the Hudson's Bay Company of the country west of the mountains. John McLoughlin had been so favourably impressed with the young Douglas that he asked him to go with him to his new charge. So instead of returning home James Douglas went to that beautiful country where he was to do so great a work.

In those days that country was ruled by the Hudson's Bay Company. The mainland part was called New Caledonia. For years the fur traders were the only Europeans there.

A few years after Douglas first went to New Caledonia, Sir George Simpson, the famous governor of the Hudson's Bay Company, visited the trading post of which he had charge. Wishing to make as great an impression as possible upon the First Nations, the governor entered Fort St. James with more than usual pomp and show. When within a mile of the fort his party stopped to have breakfast and decorate themselves. Then began the march to the fort. The British ensign was carried ahead. The buglers and bagpipers came next. The governor and a chief factor of the Company followed on horseback, and behind came the rest of the company and the baggage. When in sight of the fort the bugles sounded and the bagpipes struck up a well-known march. Upon hearing this Douglas fired a salute from his cannon and musketry and advanced to meet the governor. The greetings over, the buglers arid bagpipers paraded about to the wonder and delight of the First Nations.

Sir George Simpson was highly impressed with the ability of James Douglas, and said that he would one day be a power in the Company. He was not mistaken. Douglas did so well that the next time Simpson visited him he had risen to the second highest rank under the Hudson's Bay Company in the country west of the mountains. Later he filled a still more important position. In 1849 the Company made Fort Victoria the capital of Vancouver Island and appointed Douglas as governor. Victoria was then only a Hudson's Bay Company post, but it was built under the direction of Douglas, and was strong and well-fortified. At that time the only Europeans on the island besides the fur traders were a few farmers and miners. Up to this time the affairs of this young country had not been running quite smoothly. There had been danger of trouble with the United States over the boundary. According to agreement the boundary between the United States and what

The Father of British Columbia

is now British Columbia was the Columbia River from its mouth to the forty-ninth parallel. As time went by the United States began to claim the territory up as far as fifty-four degrees forty minutes north latitude. That was as far north as Alaska, which at that time was owned by Russia, and so the British would have been left with no Pacific coast at all. When the people of the United States began to say, "Fifty-four forty, or fight," some preparations were made for war. Fortunately, there was no fighting. The matter was settled in 1846 by the treaty of Oregon, which made the forty-ninth parallel the boundary.

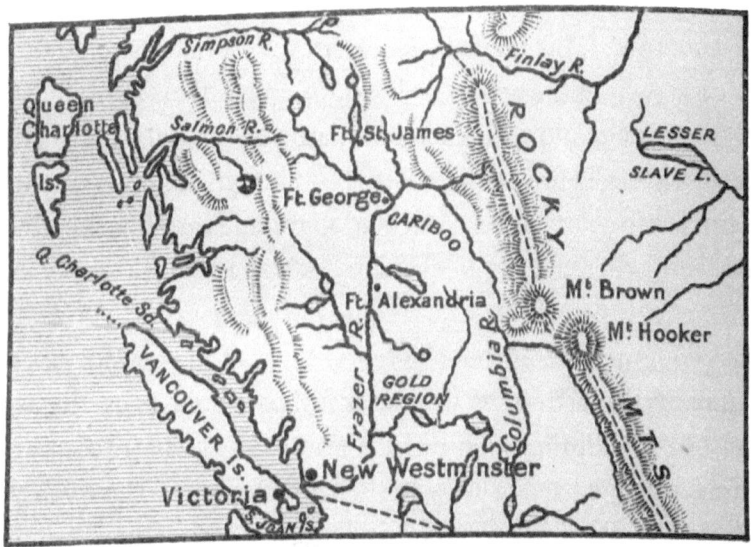

The treaty of Oregon had not made the ownership of the island of San Juan very clear. But as the Hudson's Bay Company had been there for years, the British claimed it. However, after a time the people of the United States began to claim it also. A number of them settled there and raised their flag. As the Hudson's Bay Company kept their flag up, two flags floated over the little island. During this time the United States settlers were being protected from the First Nations by the rule of the Hudson's

Bay Company. It was some time before the question of the ownership of the island was settled. The Emperor of Germany was at last asked to decide the matter, and he decided in favor of the United States.

In 1857 a sudden change came over the country under James Douglas' charge which greatly increased his work. Gold was discovered along the Fraser and Thompson Rivers, and at once there was a great rush to that district. When Governor Douglas heard of this he issued a proclamation declaring that all the gold belonged to the Crown, and that the miners might not "dig or disturb the soil" in search of it without a license or permit from the governor. This made it necessary for all miners to go first to Victoria, where the governor lived, to obtain their permits.

Victoria could not accommodate the crowds that arrived there, nor could houses be put up fast enough. Though the sound of the hammer was heard day and night and two hundred buildings were erected in six weeks, those who had even a tent to lodge in were fortunate. The little trading post soon grew to be a city of wooden houses and groups of tents. Most of the newcomers hurried on to the main-land in canoes or boats built as hastily as the houses of Victoria. Soon crowds swarmed up the Fraser River. Those who reached it early in the summer found the river high, owing to the spring freshets that came streaming down from the hills. All the sand bars were covered with deep water, so that the men could not find the gold. Some turned back in disappointment, some pushed on further into the country, but those who stayed until late in the summer when the water lowered were amply repaid.

The Father of British Columbia

Magazine illustration depicting the Fraser Canyon Gold Rush of 1858

Soda Creek, a Gold Rush town, on upper Fraser River in British Columbia (1863)

On the banks of the river the mining town of New Westminster soon sprang up. Merchants followed the miners, taking their goods up that treacherous current at great risk, and selling them at enormous prices. But even at any price it was hard to procure necessities, and many a miner realized that gold is not everything.

With the inrush of miners the work of the governor became much more difficult. Among the miners were many foreigners who knew nothing of the rule of the Hudson's Bay Company. Some were lawless characters. The governor knew that if they fought among themselves, or had any disagreement with the First Nations, much trouble and bloodshed would follow. Soon after they first began to go into the country he crossed to the mainland, and went up the Fraser River to see for himself what was going on. There he found that some were trading and mining without permits, and that speculators were taking possession of land to which they had no right and were staking lots for sale. He put a stop to these things, made laws for the people, and appointed Justices of the Peace to see that the laws were kept. Sometimes, far back in the country, it was hard to find a man who cared to act as Justice of the Peace. Once when the man to whom he offered that position objected because he felt he knew nothing of the law, the governor said, "If you know the difference between right and wrong you are qualified for the office."

When the settlers and miners began streaming into that country, the governor saw that it was no longer only a fur-trading land, and that the British Government and not the Hudson's Bay Company should rule there. About this time (1858) the Hudson's Bay Company gave up their right to rule the country west of the mountains the right which they had held since they were first granted their charter. The British Government then took it in charge. The country which had been known as New Caledonia was now called British Columbia. James Douglas, who had so ably filled the position of governor under the Hudson's Bay Company,

The Father of British Columbia

was made governor under the British Government of both British Columbia and Vancouver Island. For eight years these were separate colonies. They were then united, and Vancouver Island became a part of British Columbia.

All through the boundary troubles and the inrush of miners, Governor Douglas kept careful watch and guarded against disturbance. Under his wise rule roads were built, making it possible for settlers to go far back into the country. One of the best known of these was the Cariboo wagon road. Built along the rocky canyons and denies of the Eraser River, it extended through a country which until then had been almost impossible for the settlers to travel. This famous road opened up a region of unexpected richness for the farmer and the miner. The governor also wrote articles describing the country, so that all might know what a rich and valuable land lay west of the mountains.

Governor Douglas had a great helper in **Matthew Begbie**, who was the Chief-justice of British Columbia. In his judgments Begbie was always impartial, protecting the First Nations as carefully as he protected the Canadians. It has been said of him that he should be called the guardian rather than the judge of British Columbia.

James Douglas died in August 1877. Some years before this he had retired from the position of governor. The last years of his life were spent in rest and quiet. During that time he had taken a trip to Europe. So dearly did he love British Columbia that it was ever on his mind. Every beautiful scene abroad reminded him of some beautiful spot at home. It was while in Italy that he wrote, "A cloudy sky, a short sprinkling of rain, the low springing grass, the damp earth, and the little daisy are not unlike early March scenes in Victoria."

Part 4
Canada Under Confederation

Sir John A. Macdonald

Chapter 17
The Dominion of Canada

How Dominion Day Came

Canadians are all glad when the first of July comes, and always expect to have a good time on that day. But years ago, it was not a holiday. There was no Dominion then, so of course there could be no Dominion Day. Another great change had to be made in the government of the country before there could be a Dominion of Canada and a Canadian national holiday. We must try to understand how it all came about.

Not long after Upper and Lower Canada were joined under the Act of Union a new trouble arose. The population of Upper Canada had grown to be much greater than that of Lower Canada, and her people thought it unfair that they could not send more members to Parliament than Lower Canada. They wanted to be represented in Parliament according to their population. They said so much about "representation by population" that they had to give it the short name, "rep. by pop."

The Lower Canadians did not want "rep. by pop.," for they knew it would mean that they would not have so many members in Parliament.

Quite a bitter feeling arose between the Tories and the Reformers over "rep. by pop." Now it happened that at this time there was almost the same number of each party in Parliament, and as one side would oppose what the other side tried to do, neither party could accomplish anything. They wasted their time talking and bringing up measures that the opposite side would vote down. It was what is called a deadlock in Parliament.

All saw that if something were not done Canada would go to ruin. During this state of affairs, it was proposed in Parliament that they should try to bring about confederation that is, to unite all the provinces under one Parliament.

Seeing how much better it would be to have one great country instead of a number of separate provinces, both sides for once agreed. Though they had been bitter enemies in Parliament, they were willing to forget their strife and work for the good of their country. **John A. Macdonald** (1815-1891), the leader of the Conservative party, and **George Brown** (1818-1880), the leader of the Reform party, joined hands to work for confederation.

About this time, they heard that the men in the provinces down by the sea Nova Scotia, New Brunswick, and Prince Edward Island were thinking of uniting their provinces, and were going to have a meeting to see what could be done in the matter. The Parliament of Canada decided to send men down to this meeting to propose the union of all the provinces.

The meeting was held early in September, in the year 1864, at Charlottetown, the capital of little Prince Edward Island. As it was the first meeting, all they could do was to talk matters over and arrange for another meeting at Quebec. To Charlottetown we owe the first step in the making of the Dominion of Canada. It is called the cradle of confederation.

The meeting at Quebec was one of the most notable in Canadian history. The men who attended it spent eighteen days making out a plan of confederation. After the meeting they went about making speeches and trying to interest everyone in this great change so soon to come, the greatest change in the history of the country.

After getting the consent of the British Government, the British North America Act was passed, which was the plan of confederation made out at the Quebec meeting. It was only the Canadas,

Dominion of Canada

New Brunswick, and Nova Scotia which came into the union at this time.

The British North America Act allows each province to manage its own small matters, while the Dominion Government, in which each province is represented, has charge of the affairs which concern the whole Dominion.

Each province has a lieutenant-governor and a Parliament, and there is a governor-general and a Parliament for the Dominion. The governor-general does as the people wish. His advisers are elected by the people, and can be put out of office if they do not do right. The provinces were given "rep. by pop." in the Dominion Parliament. John A. Macdonald, who had done a very great work for confederation, was made Sir John Macdonald. He was also made first prime minister of the Dominion—that is, head of the governor's advisers.

When the British North America Act was passed, England gave up all control in Canadian affairs, except the right to forbid any act that might clash with the interests of any other part of the British Empire. This right is seldom used, for England knows that the men of Canada will pass no measure that would interfere with the welfare of any land that flies the Union Jack.

So we see that England no longer looks upon Canada as a colony to be governed, but has left her in full charge of her own affairs. The tie that now binds the Dominion to the motherland is stronger far than that of laws and rulers. It is the bond of confidence and affection.

The British North America Act came into force on July 1, 1867. That was the birthday of the Dominion, a new holiday which Canadians have celebrated ever since. It is the day when they close their schools and their places of business and raise their national flag; a day when all true Canadians should remember with gratitude those Fathers of Confederation who set aside party strife and united to make Canada,

> "A band of scattered huts and colonies no more,
> But a young nation, with her life full beating in her breast,
> A noble future in her eyes—the Britain of the West."

The Dominion Extended

The Fathers of Confederation hoped that all the provinces would join the Dominion. They soon had the satisfaction of seeing the great northwest united with Canada. This was accomplished by paying the Hudson's Bay Company, which still had the right to that country, a large sum of money and allowing them to have a piece of land round each of their trading posts, and to continue their fur trade.

The arrangements were made, and all went well as far as the Hudson's Bay Company were concerned. But a misunderstanding arose with the Métis who lived there. The new arrangement was not to come into effect until January 1870, but during the summer of 1869 surveyors went out and began measuring the land and dividing it into lots.

Many of the surveyors gave the settlers a wrong idea of the change which was being made. When the Métis saw them at work, driving stakes and dividing the land into square lots, they were frightened, for they thought that their land might be taken from them. About this time the man who had been appointed by the Canadian Government to be governor of that country when the new arrangements came into effect set out for Fort Garry. News of this reached the Métis, and they became still more alarmed.

Dominion of Canada

Now at this time lived **Louis Riel** (1844-1885), who was one of the best educated among the Métis. He had made himself their leader. It was not hard for him to do this, as he was a clever speaker, and had great influence over his people. When he heard that a governor was really on the way to them, he induced them to unite to keep this new governor out of the country.

Councillors of the Provisional Government of the Métis Nation, with Louis Riel in direct centre

The first thing they did was to build a fence across the road by which the governor would come into the settlement. When **Governor William McDougall** (1822–1905) arrived with his family, tired after the long journey, he found that, instead of a welcome, a fence guarded by angry Métis had been prepared for his reception. When ordered to remove the fence the Métis refused. As they were well armed, Mr. McDougall's party was obliged to retreat to Pembina, the fort that had so often been the refuge of Lord Selkirk's colonists.

Riel now took possession of Fort Garry. He talked much of what he would do for his people, and it was no wonder that the Métis looked upon him as their protector. Meanwhile, Mr. McDougall and his family were having a hard time at Pembina, for they had not been expected there, and found no comforts.

Wishing to frighten the Canadians who stood out against him, Riel arrested **Dr. John Schultz** (1840–1896), his political rival, and some of his followers and shut them up in Fort Garry. One day when Schultz was wondering whether he was ever to get out again, one of his friends sent him a pudding. Deep down in the centre he found a knife and a gimlet. At once he cut the buffalo robe he slept on into long strips, and tied them together to serve as a rope. It was not long enough, so he cut up some of his clothes as well. When night came he fastened one end to the window-casing by means of the gimlet and let himself down. Only partly clad, he made his escape in a cold January storm. Riel afterwards set the others free.

Now, as you know, all this happened before the Canadian Government had taken over the control of the country. The Hudson's Bay Company governor was ill, and when these troubles arose he told them to form some government, for he could do nothing. So Riel continued to rule. Matters remained quiet until a party marched in from Portage la Prairie and were taken prisoners by him. Then, determined to frighten those who opposed him, he had one young Canadian among them, Thomas Scott, condemned to death. Nothing could turn Riel from his cruel purpose. All entreaty was in vain. One dreary March day Scott was led out under the wall of Fort Garry and shot. His body was refused to his friends, and what was done with it has never been known.

Dominion of Canada

When tidings of the shooting of Scott spread through Canada there was great sorrow and indignation. Canadians gladly volunteered to march against Riel and his followers.

Soon Colonel Wolseley set out with a force for the long, tiresome journey. There was no railway to the prairies then, and they were obliged to follow the fur traders' route, which gave them hundreds and hundreds of miles of rough land to travel over.

Riel had declared that he wished only to retain power until he could hand it over to a proper government. But when he heard that troops were coming he fled to the United States. Most of his followers went back to their homes. By this time Bishop Tache, priest of St. Boniface, who had been away, was back again. He assured his people that their homes would not be taken from them, and helped them to understand the change which was taking place in the government of the country.

The Manitoba Act was now passed, forming the province of Manitoba, and giving it a government like that of Ontario. Governor Archibald was sent out instead of Governor McDougall, whose going too soon had been misunderstood by the Métis. The Lieutenant-governor of Manitoba was also made Governor of the North-West Territories. And so in 1870 the rule of the Hudson's Bay Company in that land was at an end.

Thirty-five years later, in 1905, two provinces were formed out of the North-West Territories, and each of these provinces was given a lieutenant-governor and a Parliament of its own. The provinces were called Alberta and Saskatchewan.

The Fathers of Confederation were grieved that Manitoba, Alberta, and Saskatchewan, in becoming a part of the Dominion, should have caused disturbance. But the next year their hearts were gladdened by the union with them of the far-distant province of British Columbia. Their fond hopes were realized now; the Dominion extended from sea to sea.

When British Columbia joined the Dominion the Canadian Government promised to build a railway right across the country to the Pacific Coast, thus connecting British Columbia with the Eastern Provinces.

Strange to say, little Prince Edward Island, whose capital had been the cradle of confederation, came into the union last. This province had one great trouble. Rich men from other countries owned nearly all the island, and those who worked the land could not have it as their own and do as they wished with it. The Dominion Government promised this little province, when she joined with them, to help her out of her difficulty by buying out the rich landowners and giving the inhabitants a chance to own their homes.

Newfoundland was still an outsider for quite some time.[2] England's "oldest colony" was the last to join the Dominion. For many years she was very much like an outsider, too, for she has a foreign shore; that is to say, French fishermen had a right to land along her western coast.

Though that is no longer the case, for many years the island out in the foggy gulf preferred to remain alone with her fisheries.

---

[2] Newfoundland and Labrador joined Canada in 1949.

Chapter 18
The Canadian West

The Governors and the First Nations

In the days when the country west of the Great Lakes was under the rule of the Hudson's Bay Company, the First Nation had it all for their hunting-grounds, except that small part where the Selkirk settlers were living. But when the West passed out of the hands of the Hudson's Bay Company, the hunting-grounds were gradually changed into farm lands, and towns took the place of the trading posts. To the First Nations, this was an unfair situation. What right had the Europeans to come and take away their land and make it something different?

Then the Government made treaties or agreements with them, much like the treaty Lord Selkirk had made with the First Nations who had lived on the land he bought for his colony. By these treaties the Government granted the First Nations great reserves of land in return for their giving up the country to the Canadians. On these reserves they might have their homes and live as they wished. The Government also promised to give them farm implements and to teach them how to farm.

At such a time there was need of strong men in that country-men who understood the First Nations and who were trusted by them. Such men could go among them and speak for the Government, and explain the meaning of the treaties so that all the First Nations would thoroughly understand them.

Fortunately there were men who could do this. They were the men who were the Lieutenant-governors of Manitoba and the North-West Territories during the years in which the treaties were being made.

When each treaty was signed the governor went out and held a meeting with the First Nations who were to be included in the treaty. Most of the treaties were signed by the First Nations during the time in which Alexander Morris was Lieutenant-governor. These words from his speech at one of the meetings show how he expressed himself to the First Nations:

> I am here to tell you all the Queen's mind; but recollect this. The Queen's High Councillor here from Ottawa, and I, her governor, are not traders; we do not come here in the spirit of traders; we come here to tell you openly, without hiding anything, just what the Queen will do for you…The promises we have to make will be carried out as long as the sun shines above and the water flows in the ocean. When you are ready to plant seed the Queen's men will lay off reserves so as to give a square mile to every family of five persons, and on commencing to farm the Queen will give to every family cultivating the soil two hoes, one spade, one scythe for cutting the grain, one axe and plough, enough of seed wheat, barley, oats, and potatoes to plant the land they get ready. The Queen wishes her red children to learn the cunning of the white man, and when they are ready for it she will send schoolmasters to every reserve and pay them.

The Canadian West

Royal Canadian Mounted Policeman

Mounted Policemen

There was another work for which brave men were needed in the West. That was the work of the Mounted Policemen. They were the guardians of the plains, whose duty it was to keep order and see that the laws were kept. At this time there were only a little over two hundred Mounted Policemen for all that great country.

As more and more settlers came their work became harder. The buffaloes were fast disappearing, and so the First Nations were dissatisfied and restless. Lawless traders were bringing liquor into the country and selling it to the poor First Nations, to ill effect. That there was so little trouble in the country at such a time is due to the guardians of the plains. Many were the adventures which they had in trying to make the First Nations understand that they must keep the British laws.

Colonel Denny, one of the first of the Mounted Police force, tells how at one time a message was brought to him, that at Blackfoot Crossing a Cree man had been killed by a Blackfoot man, and the Cree were going to have their revenge by attacking the Blackfoot camp.

Now he knew that this would mean bloodshed and massacre, perhaps the beginning of long warfare among the First Nations. As a Mounted Policeman it was his duty to prevent it. Only six men could be spared, but with those six and an interpreter he started for the crossing. After a long, hard journey they came to the camp on a bluff overlooking the river. It consisted of about one thousand Blackfoot warriors. Three miles away was the Cree camp of the same number.

Colonel Denny went at once to the Blackfoot camp to arrest the murderer, but found that he had escaped. The Blackfoot were angry with the Cree, and declared that there were good reasons for the murder. But Colonel Denny told them that they must make peace. "Put up a lodge in which to hold a peace meeting," he said, "and I will bring the Cree chiefs over."

Then he went to the Cree camp. The Cree were even more angry than the Blackfoot, but after he had talked with them they were willing to listen to reason, and promised to attend the meeting.

The next morning Colonel Denny and his interpreter went to the tent the Blackfoot had put up for the peace meeting. Soon Crowfoot, the great chief of the Blackfoot, came, paced about the fire with great ceremony, shook hands, and presented the Mounted Policeman with a beautiful buffalo robe. Then over thirty chiefs, both Cree and Blackfoot, came in. Each shook hands and each presented him with a buffalo robe, so he now had a great pile of robes.

After this the peace pipe was smoked in grave silence as was their custom. Then Colonel Denny made a long speech. The First Nations listened attentively, and no angry glances were cast at one another. He told them that their great mother, the Queen across the ocean, wished them to live at peace with one another. Since the murderer had escaped, he advised the Blackfoot to settle by paying so many horses to the family of the murdered man. He also advised the Cree to go quietly back to their own country.

But they did not decide quickly. For hours they sat and listened to the speeches of the chiefs, telling their grievances. After a great deal of talk they promised to do as he advised. The Blackfoot promised that if the murderer ever came back they would hand him over to the police.

Then after again shaking hands all around the meeting was over, and Colonel Denny was able to return.

This is only one of the stories which tell how bloodshed among the First Nations was prevented by the Mounted Policemen.

Six Blackfoot Chiefs by Paul Kane

The Saskatchewan Rebellion (1885)

Great changes had taken place in Manitoba since the trouble at Red River. People were beginning to know what a fertile farming country the great prairie land was, and settlers were pouring in both from Eastern Canada and from other countries. Even the Mennonites from Southern Russia had found their way there. The capital of Manitoba was now the great thriving town of Winnipeg, which was very different from little Fort Garry of the days when the province was first formed.

The Canadian West

The growth in population was found not only in Manitoba, but extended to the North-West Territory beyond. Many of the Métis had left Manitoba and settled on the Saskatchewan River. There they had long narrow farms, much like the farms of the French-Canadians on the St. Lawrence, and there they lived happy lives. When the settlers began to take up land there too, the Métis and First Nations became upset, for they saw that the game was being driven farther and farther away. Some of the settlers were careless hunters, who shot down many more buffaloes than they needed and frightened away the herds. And so the First Nations and Métis began to fear that a time would come when there would be no buffaloes to hunt, and they would have no more "pemmican." This was their chief food; it was made by pounding and drying the buffalo meat.

When the surveyors reached the Saskatchewan, and began dividing the land there into square farms, the Métis became alarmed. These men went to their very homes, drove stakes here and there upon their land, and were changing the long narrow farms into square ones, which did not at all suit the Métis' way of living. They did not see why the men could not go and survey on the great tract of land where there were no settlers to be disturbed, and they feared they would lose their farms altogether. It was the Red River trouble over again.

The Métis had no representatives or members in the Parliament at Ottawa to plead their cause, but they sent petitions to the Dominion Government asking for title-deeds to their lands, such as had been given to their people who had remained in Manitoba. These title-deeds would give them the legal right to their farms, so that they could not be taken from them.

At Ottawa the matter was put aside for a time. When the Métis received no reply to their petitions, they sent for their old friend Louis Riel. Riel was teaching in a school in the United States; but his time of banishment from Canada was up, and he came to them at once.

By the spring of 1885 Riel had made his headquarters at Batoche, and was gathering the Métis together for rebellion. But, more alarming than all, he was trying to arouse the First Nations, who were living quietly on their reserves. Had they listened to him, and gone on the war-path, it would have been the most terrible thing that could have happened to the settlers. To oppose Riel and his followers there were only a little band of settlers, and a few hundred Mounted Police who had been left there to keep order. The First Nations and Métis could easily have swept them away; so it is little wonder that there was great alarm in the settlements.

Now it happened that some provisions and ammunition were stored at Duck Lake, not far from Batoche. When a party set out to secure these, they arrived only to find **Gabriel Dumont** (1837–1906), Riel's helper, and a force of Métis there before them. They hurried back for reinforcements; but even then they were far outnumbered by the Métis, who fired on them from behind bushes and trees. Twelve of the settlers were killed, and they were obliged to retreat.

The Government now realized that they had delayed too long in considering the case of the Métis, and that the result was a rebellion. Canadian volunteers responded willingly to the call to arms, and soon a large force under **General Frederick Middleton** (1825–1898) was on its way to the Saskatchewan. The railway which was being built across the continent did not yet reach so far west as the troops must go, and they had to travel on foot or on horseback over great stretches of bleak country through the snow and rain of early spring.

The Canadian West

Photograph of Big Bear (standing fourth from left) and other Cree trading at Fort Pitt, Saskatchewan in 1884

While the soldiers were enduring the hardships of the journey, **Big Bear** (1825–1888), a Cree chieftain, was causing much trouble. Big Bear, it seems, had dreamed dreams, and he had great faith in his dreams. He had dreamed of disease, and smallpox had come to his people. He had dreamed of famine, and famine had come. It came when the buffaloes were gone, and the settlers were turning the hunting-grounds into farm lands. Then he had dreamed of war, and directly Riel began urging him to take up arms, and help to drive away the settlers who were causing so much trouble. Big Bear stopped to think of the good old days when no Europeans were farming on the hunting-grounds, and herds of buffaloes dotted the plains. While he was thinking of these things Riel told him that the Great Manitou was working with him, and on a certain day in March would give a sign from the sky by darkening the sun. This would be a signal for them to go on the war-path. Big Bear watched, and on that very day the sun did darken. It was an eclipse which Riel knew would take place. But Big Bear knew nothing about an eclipse; and, as he watched the sun darken, he felt that it must be as Riel said, a sign from the Great Spirit.

After this, Big Bear gathered his warriors together, swooped down upon the little settlement of Frog Lake, and killed or took as prisoners all the settlers who were there. The Métis, however, gave up their horses to get the women away from the Cree.

Big Bear then hurried down to Fort Pitt, which was guarded by only twenty-three Mounted Police, commanded by Francis Dickens, a son of the great English novelist. They held out as long as they could, then destroyed their ammunition and food and retreated down the river to Battleford.

The settlers were terribly alarmed now. To increase their distress, the telegraph wires were down, and they could not send word of their position or find out how near help was.

But the soldiers were approaching as fast as the terrible roads would permit. They were now divided into three sections. One under General Strange was sent against Big Bear, another under Colonel Otter to Battleford, and the third General Middleton led to Batoche, Riel's stronghold.

The force under General Strange followed Big Bear for many weeks, and at last came up with him, and succeeded in getting the prisoners away from him.

When the force under Colonel Otter reached Battleford, they found the settlers who had gathered there in a terrible state of alarm. They were all fearing that **Poundmaker** (1842-1886), a Cree chief who was on his reserve a few miles away, was going to attack them. Now Poundmaker was a fine man, and had no intention of doing anything of the kind. But as he had heard so much

The Canadian West

talk of soldiers and of war, he thought he had better be ready, so that if his people should be attacked they could defend their wives and their babies. This was why he had taken up a strong position on a mound beside Cut Knife Creek. Some of the Cree who were with him had stolen away to Battleford, and pillaged and burned houses, and had even shot two men; all these things had terrified the people there.

When Colonel Otter arrived at Battleford with his soldiers, he determined to put a stop to further trouble from that band of First Nations. He marched out to Cut Knife Creek and attacked Poundmaker. The chief and his warriors fought bravely in defence of their people, and the soldiers were obliged to retreat. Poundmaker said afterwards that he would never have fought had he not been first attacked.

General Middleton met the enemy before he reached Batoche. As he marched quietly along the Saskatchewan River, with his men divided, so that half were on one side and half on the other, he came upon Dumont with a force at Fish Creek, a tributary of the Saskatchewan. At once the soldiers on the other side began to cross the river. But they had only one small boat, and many were not able to cross until the attack was over. There was a sharp fight before the Métis were driven back. The loss was heavy in General Middleton's army, and, realizing that the enemy was not to be trifled with, he decided to wait reinforcements before going on to Batoche.

General Middleton remained where he was until the ice broke up, and a small steamer, the *Northcote* arrived with reinforcements. The *Northcote* was then turned into a gun-boat, and the army moved on to Batoche, reaching there on May 9. The Métis had trenches all round. Middleton camped about half a mile away.

It was three days before Batoche was captured. Though a continual firing was kept up, little was done except skirmishing until the third day. On that day a charge was made, the Métis were driven out of Batoche, and Riel's prisoners were set free. Dumont, whose skilful fighting had won the admiration of the Canadian volunteers, made his escape to the United States. Riel was taken prisoner.

After the battle of Batoche, Middleton moved on to Battleford. There he met Poundmaker, who had come in to make his surrender. This was the most remarkable meeting which ever took place in the Canadian West. The First Nations, ornamented with feathers and paint and bits of European finery, sat about upon the ground in a great semicircle, and in front of them was the greatest force of soldiers that had ever gathered in that country. Speeches were made by the chiefs and the general, through his interpreter. Poundmaker and the man who had shot the settlers were taken prisoners. Poundmaker was afterwards tried, and though in his defense he said, "Everything I did was done to stop bloodshed," he was sentenced to imprisonment. But through the influence of those who knew him, he was released before his time was up. Eight Cree men were found guilty of murder and hanged. Riel was tried for treason and hanged at Regina. His friends buried his body in the graveyard of St. Boniface at Winnipeg.

Too much credit cannot be given to those who went among the First Nations during the spring of 1885 and induced them to remain at peace. Much was done in this way by the missionaries and the Mounted Police.

The rebellion drew the attention of the Canadian Government to the North-West. Title-deeds were now granted to the Métis. The North-West Territory, which before the rebellion had been divided into Athabasca, Alberta, Assiniboia, and Saskatchewan, was allowed to send members to the Dominion Parliament. The number of Mounted Police was increased to one thousand. There has been no trouble since. The rebellion has been followed by years of steady progress throughout the prairie land.

Poundmaker and his wife

The Railway across the Continent

When British Columbia joined the Dominion, the Canadian Government promised to build the railway to the Pacific coast within ten years, but it was not finished quite so soon. It was no easy matter to build a railway from Montreal to Vancouver, a distance of almost three thousand miles, and through a country of which, at that time, great stretches were quite unsettled. There were many difficulties in starting such a great work. Choosing the best place to lay the track was an undertaking in itself.

The chief difficulty was not in the prairie land, but at the great mountains. Even there all obstacles were overcome by the skillful workmen. Tunnels were cut through rock, and trestle-work was made to bridge the great ravines.

In many places snow-sheds were built above the track to protect it from the masses of melting snow and ice that would at times come pouring down the mountain sides.

The railway was begun from each end, and the two lines were built towards each other. In November 1885 they met at the lonely little station of Craigellachie, beside the Eagle River, in the Rocky Mountains. The last spike was driven by Sir Donald Smith, who is now Lord Strathcona.

Settlers, instead of going across the country in "prairie schooners," as the covered wagons were called in which they used to travel to the West, ride in fast trains and view the glorious scenery among the snow-capped mountains from the observation car; and where, before the days of the railway, only wild animals roamed, flourishing towns and villages are now to be seen.

This famous railway opened up to us valuable lands, connected the East with the rich province of British Columbia, and, by extending to Vancouver, where boats sail for China, it has given us the long-talked-of, long-searched-for North-West Passage, though not a water route such as Cartier, Champlain, La Salle, and poor Henry Hudson hoped to find.

The Canadian Pacific will always be famous as the first line to cross the continent and pass the great mountains. But it was not the only one for long. The Grand Trunk Pacific and the Canadian Northern built their railways from sea to sea.

Chapter 19
The Canada of Today

A Long Journey

Suppose you start for a make-believe journey through Canada and see it as it is today. Now, if you are ready, pretend that you are going on the most wonderful airplane imaginable, and that it takes you from one place to another as quickly as you can think.

You visit the farmers first, for farming, you know, is the chief work of the people of Canada. You will see them in every province, and you are almost sure to find them busy. They raise many different kinds of grain, but more wheat than anything else. Manitoba is the most noted wheat-growing district. When you notice the comfortable homes and great fields of grain, you cannot help thinking of the hardships of the Selkirk settlers who were the first farmers in that country.

One thing that may surprise you in that part is that you see no fences along the roadsides. If you could stay until harvest time you would see how beautiful the country looks with its great unbroken stretches of yellow grain.

If you leave your airplane long enough to walk through some Canadian pasture-fields, you will find some fine cattle, horses, and sheep. Canada is well adapted for stock-raising. Even in the West, where herds of buffaloes used to roam, there are now great cattle ranches. The cattle there are branded or marked with the mark of the ranch to which they belong, and allowed to run wild. Twice a year the rancher gathers them together to count them and mark the young ones. This is called the "round-up."

Horses, the broncos of the West, run wild, too, until caught and trained by the cowboys. In time they become most intelligent, useful animals, and, in their own way, as skillful as their riders.

Besides his grain and cattle, the farmer has his dairy work and poultry, and, if he does not live too far north, his fruit, to keep him busy.

You say good-bye to him now, for, though he answers carefully all your questions, you know that his time is very precious.

Image from 1882 magazine

A Lumber Camp

You call for a few moments at Montreal, where all through the summer great ocean vessels come and go. There you see that shipload after shipload of Canadian grain sails away to feed the world. Shiploads of apples too are going, and even butter, eggs, and small fruits are carried. The cold-storage department of the ships keeps these things ice-cold, so that they arrive perfectly fresh.

Now that you are at Montreal you might go up the Ottawa River and visit the lumbermen. You will have to go far up the river to find them at work. The forest scenes are very different from those long ago of which you have read. Then the settler chopped down the trees and burned them to make a clearing about his cabin, but now the logs are carefully floated down the lakes and rivers to the sawmills.

The men tell you that the ground is frozen so hard in winter that no matter how swampy it is in the forest they can work. Some are employed all winter in cutting down trees, others in making roads over which the logs are drawn to the nearest creek or river. At night the men sleep in the little shanties they have built for themselves.

Lumber Raft by Frances Anne Hopkins (1868)

Timber Rafts

Let us suppose that your visit falls in the springtime. The ice has broken up, and the logs are being floated down the swollen streams. It is dangerous work, especially at the rapids, where there is always risk of a log being caught, stopping the others, and causing what the men call a jam. When that happens, the men jump from one log to another trying with their long poles to loosen the logs and start them all moving again. You would wonder, if you saw them, how they keep from slipping into the water, and you would realize that were it not for the bravery of these men, who work amid such dangers, the lumber industry of our country could not be carried on.

To float the logs down the large rivers they bind them together and make a raft, and at the lakes a tug is waiting to tow them along. Suppose you follow as far as the sawmills, where the logs are made into lumber for shipment or home use. The men tell you that the greatest quantity shipped goes to England, and those who understand the lumbering business in the different parts of Canada say that the river Ottawa and the river St. John in New Brunswick are two of the greatest of Canadian lumbering rivers.

If you have time to glance at the large factories on the lakes and rivers, you will see the lumber being turned into furniture. Pianos, organs, and farm implements are also manufactured. The newest factories are where wood pulp is made a material which was unknown in Canada years ago, and which is produced from spruce and poplar trees. Paper, tubs, pails, and many other useful articles are made out of it. Canada can now use her own paper for books and newspapers, and have quantities left to sell to other countries.

On your visit to the fisheries you learn something you must never forget, that Canada contains the most valuable fisheries in the world. The ships that now carry our fish away to be sold in other countries are a great contrast to the strange little vessels of the early fishermen of the days of Cartier, who braved the dangers

The Canada of Today

of the almost unknown waters and made a beginning in this great industry.

The oldest fisheries of Canada are those of the Gulf of St. Lawrence and the Bay of Fundy, where cod, herring, lobsters, and the oysters you all like so much are found in great quantities. You will find fishermen on the shores of the Great Lakes too, who tell us that they make a good living by fishing. They are so skillful in managing their boats that we see them going out to their nets, though the water is rough and the weather dark and stormy.

The most wonderful fisheries of all are the salmon fisheries of British Columbia. You may remember buying cans marked Columbia or Fraser River salmon. On the shores of these rivers you see large factories where they are canned. The men at work there will tell you many stories of these rivers. Among other things they tell you that at some seasons the fish are so numerous that they can be caught in the hands, and that far back in lonely places they have seen bears walk into the river and dine sumptuously on choice salmon.

As you have many visits to make, you must bid goodbye to the fisheries, but not until you have tasted some delicious salmon, for you are invited to dine at a beautiful place overlooking the Columbia River.

You see many schools as you travel about, and you pass by colleges and universities too. One college is some distance out from Toronto, with fields and orchards about it. This, you learn, is the Ontario Agricultural College. You are told that there are agricultural schools in the other provinces also. The farmers are glad of such colleges and schools, for there the students learn how best to care for the stock, how to destroy insects that eat grain, the most approved way of working the soil, and many other things important on the farm.

You are quite surprised at the number of railways you look down upon. If you make inquiries you will be told that there are over 26,000 miles of railway in Canada, and more have already been arranged for. The land where the buffalo roamed and the First Nations plied their canoes has become a network of railway lines. In this way the riches of Canada have been opened up to all.

The canals, too, have been greatly improved. They have been made deeper, and new ones have been built. There is now a great canal to pass the falls of Sault Ste. Marie, between Lake Superior and Lake Huron, and large vessels can sail from Lake Superior through the Great Lakes and their connecting rivers to the St. Lawrence River, and thence to the sea. You would like to take that trip some time, but you know it would take much longer than the journey on your airplane.

You notice a telephone office at almost every place where you stop. At many of the farmhouses also there are telephones. You wish to know who invented such a great convenience, and you ask an old gentleman who seems to take a great interest in the country.

"The telephone belongs to Canada," he proudly tells you. "It was invented by **Alexander Graham Bell**, and the first telephone to be used was a trial line put up between his house and that of a neighbor in Brantford, Ontario."

As you have travelled so far over the country, you now leave the remainder of your journey for another day. While resting you think over what you have seen and heard, so that you will not forget it.

Once more you are aboard your airplane. Suppose you go to the mines this time, for that is where Canada gets a large part of her wealth. Coal, iron, lead, copper, cobalt, nickel, gold, silver, lime, salt, asbestos, gypsum, and petroleum are all found in the

The Canada of Today

Dominion. Petroleum is found in the south-western part of Ontario, and in the northern part of this province valuable minerals are found, among others gold. In Quebec you see excellent iron mines, and in Nova Scotia are famous coal mines. But British Columbia is the most valuable mining province of Canada. Great riches have been found there since gold was first discovered along the river banks, and hundreds of miners are at work.

You hear so much about the Klondike goldfields in the Yukon territory, to the north of British Columbia, that you will put on your furs and steer your airplane northwards. The miners there are searching for gold in the beds and along the banks of the rivers and up on the hillsides in the beds of the streams now dry.

If you can find an old miner who has time to talk, he will tell you that in spite of the hardships of the journey hundreds and thousands of miners travelled there some years ago, and Dawson City sprang up. It was composed at first of huts and tents, for men came in crowds before houses could be built.

For nine months in the year the Yukon River is frozen over, and as there was no railway, during that time all goods had to be carried over the terrible mountain passes and taken on to Dawson on sleighs drawn by dogs or men. For that reason, food was very expensive. Only the plainest could be had at all, and sometimes not enough of that. Many a miner with bags of gold dust knew what it was to live on one "flapjack" a day.

*The headquarters of the Trading & Exploring Co.,
Dawson City, Yukon (1899)*

But you see that Dawson has improved within these few years. There is a telegraph line reaching there now, and houses have taken the place of huts and tents. Though the country is rich in gold, and panfuls of earth have been taken out which contained hundreds of dollars' worth of gold dust and nuggets, there are some unfortunate men who spend all they have and come away poor.

You notice a great many dogs in the Klondike, and the miners tell you that they are of the greatest aid. They do not look like the dogs you have seen. They are the native dogs of the north, and resemble the wolf in appearance, having the same short-pointed

The Canada of Today

ears and slanting eyes. They sleep out in the streets in the snow, their thick coats protecting them from the severest cold.

They are not made pets of as our dogs are. There is little time for that in the cold north. The dogs there are busy creatures, and take the place of horses. You see them hauling wood and supplies, and even carrying the mail. It is wonderful what loads they can draw. They are harnessed, not side by side, but one in front of the other. Usually there are five for each load.

Their owners tell you that they endure cold and hunger remarkably well, and that almost the only care they need is to be allowed to go into the tent to dry their feet. If their feet become sore, sometimes their masters make moccasins for them with leather soles and cloth tops. The dogs soon learn that these protect their feet from hard rough snow and ice, and will often coax to have them put on.

During the summer months, when the ground is bare, the dogs carry small loads on their backs as packhorses do. Valuable loads they are, too, sometimes, for many a dog has helped to carry his master's gold dust. Nowhere in your travels have you found this faithful animal more necessary than in the northern part of Canada.

While in the north, you see some Indigenous people with packs of furs. They travel along very quickly, and if you follow you will find that they soon reach a queer little fort on the river bank with the Hudson's Bay Company flag floating above it. So you know that it is a Hudson's Bay Company trading post. The workers there are trading with them for their furs. One Indigenous man is getting some flour and tea, a small parcel of sugar, which he holds very carefully, and a little coat for his boy, which will be a great change from the rabbit-skin clothes the mother has made for him. Then the trader gives him a gay-coloured scarf, which evidently pleases him greatly.

You know from what you have seen that the fur trade is still carried on, though much farther north than it was years ago, for the settling of the country has driven the fur-bearing animals nearer the Arctic regions.

Meeting with the Indigenous peoples reminds you that you should visit the First Nations whose ancestors filled such an important place in Canada's history long ago.

You find them no longer lords of the forest, the lake, and the stream, and no longer carrying the tomahawk. Except in the far north, the few that are left live on land set apart by the Government. Some of them farm in a small way. There are schools in the settlement, and churches, too, and missionaries to preach to them. Many of the First Nations belong to the Christian church, though some still follow their own religion.

Even in the far north the missionaries go among them and establish schools. They teach the First Nations many useful things, among others how to make gardens. They tell you that growth in the north is so rapid that, though there are only a few months of summer, potatoes and other vegetables are raised, and that even on the Arctic coast, where the summer is only six weeks long, radishes are grown successfully. The person who learns to grow potatoes has a means of supplying himself with food when fish and game are scarce.

It is very pleasant to come upon a mission school surrounded by its garden in that lonely, dreary land. Even on the Arctic coast there are missionaries who have left the comforts of home and taken that lonely trip on snow-shoes or in dog trains to the land of the long night, to carry their religion to the First Nations and the Inuit.

The Canada of Today

The missionaries of the north have many hardships, and they find much that is new to them. Skins are put to many uses in that country. At a bright little mission school where you stay for dinner you are told a true story of a church near Great Slave Lake. This little church was made of moose skins, and was eaten up one night by some hungry dogs. But now it is growing late, and you must go home.

As you turn your airplane homeward, suppose you think over what is most important in each of Canada's provinces, so that you will never forget it.

Ontario is called the leading province of Canada, but only during recent years has the great importance of her northern districts been known. British Columbia is one of the foremost provinces in mining importance. With such valuable minerals, fisheries, and farm lands, a delightful climate and glorious scenery amidst the snow-capped mountains, it is a province the Dominion is proud to claim.

British Columbia

You will never forget the wheat fields that have made Manitoba and Saskatchewan and Alberta so noted, and have drawn men from many different countries. Winnipeg, the capital of Manitoba, shows how that part has grown in population. In Riel's day it was little Fort Garry, with only a few houses, and now it is a great and flourishing city.

Manitoba

The St. Lawrence River makes Quebec an important part of the Dominion. Montreal, where the ocean steamers come and go until the river is frozen over in winter, is the second-largest and busiest city of Canada. The majority of French-Canadians still cling to their old customs and language. In many a little village you hear the French language spoken just as it was spoken there when the *fleur-de-lis* waved over the capital.

The Canada of Today

Château Frontenac in Modern-day Quebec

Little Prince Edward Island, though the smallest province, is the most thickly populated for its size. The climate is mild, much like that of England, and the inhabitants are happy and prosperous.

Prince Edward Island

New Brunswick is not so thickly settled as most of the other provinces. It still has many great forests, which make it most noted for lumbering. St. John, one of the ports of New Brunswick, has for some time ranked third among the seaports of Canada. In the winter, when the St. Lawrence is frozen over, it is our chief shipping port.

New Brunswick

Nova Scotia is the first province in fishing importance. This is not to be wondered at, since it is situated in the midst of Canada's oldest fisheries, and has so much coast-line for its size, and so many sheltered ports for the fishermen. It is a great mining province as well. In Cape Breton, which is part of Nova Scotia, there are large steel and iron works. The old historic Louisburg, where Wolfe won his first great Canadian victory, may one day be a great winter port.

As you pass over the great island of Newfoundland and Labrador, the last of the provinces to join this large nation, at last

The Canada of Today

your journey is over. Canada today has ten provinces: Alberta, British Columbia, Manitoba, New Brunswick, Newfoundland and Labrador, Nova Scotia, Ontario, Prince Edward Island, Quebec, and Saskatchewan, and three territories: Northwest Territories, Nunavut, and Yukon.

Chapter 20
Our Country and Our Flag

Canada's emblem is the Maple Leaf, but her flag was once that of the British Empire, the Union Jack.[3] It has a story of its own. Years ago it was not a Union Jack, for then it was only the cross of England. But when the crowns of England and Scotland united, the cross of the Scottish flag was added; and later, over a hundred years ago, the cross of the Irish flag was placed there also, making the present Union Jack. In Canada the Canadian coat-of-arms was placed in the flag.

Canada's maple leaf flag

---

[3] The current Canadian maple leaf flag was adopted in 1965.

This flag has waved over the pioneers who cut down the forest trees and opened the way for those who followed, and has waved over the soldiers who, in the days gone by, fought against an invading enemy. It has seen great changes in the government of the country from the day it first floated over the citadel of Quebec to the grandest achievement of all, the confederation of the provinces.

It has been through all the years a flag of freedom and justice, and it is little wonder we fly our colors with proud hearts.

> It's only a small bit of bunting,
> It's only an old colored rag;
> Yet thousands have died for its honor,
> And shed their best blood for the flag.
> You may say it's an old bit of bunting,
> You may say it's an old colored rag;
> But Freedom has made it majestic,
> And time has ennobled the flag.

Our Country and Our Flag

In January 1901 the good Queen Victoria, who, beloved of all her subjects, had ruled over the British Empire for more than sixty years, passed away, and Albert Edward, Prince of Wales, became King Edward the Seventh. At his death, in 1910, George the Fifth came to the throne.

In 1911 Canada was highly favored. A member of the royal family, His Royal Highness the Duke of Connaught, a son of the great Queen Victoria, came to Canada as Governor-General. From the day of his arrival his broad sympathies were felt throughout the Dominion. Far and near, Canadians were inspired by his presence in their land.

As we look back over the history of Canada, it is hard to realize that the land on which the European man first set foot, but little over four hundred years ago, is now a nation of happy, prosperous people. To the noble men and women who have lived before us, and who live today, we owe Canada's progress and Canada's greatness.

Soon the school children will be men and women, and their country will be in their keeping. May they be as brave and noble as those who made Canada what she is, honoring the Maple Leaf and the Union Jack, and leaving to those who come after, an example of true loyalty. Thus may they do their part in guiding their country, ever onward and upward, through the years to come.

Image Attribution

Pg. 18
Maquette du village d'Hochelaga by Pierre5018 (https://commons.wikimedia.org/wiki/File:Maquette_du_village_d%27Hochelaga.jpg)

Pg. 20
Rekonstruktion eines Huron-Langhauses (im Ojibwa-Museum in St. Ignace) By KiwiDeaPi at German Wikipedia (https://commons.wikimedia.org/wiki/File:Huron-Langhaus.jpg)

Pg. 37
Quebec- Champlain Monument by Dennis Jarvis from Halifax, Canada (https://commons.wikimedia.org/wiki/File:Quebec_DSC08620_-_Champlain_Monument_(36997471655).jpg)

Pg. 38
Jean de Brébeuf with the Huron (Stained glass) in Martyr`s Shrine in Midland, Ontario by Mykola Swarnyk (https://commons.wikimedia.org/wiki/File:Jean_de_Br%C3%A9beuf_Midland,_Ontario.jpg)

Pg. 94
United Empire Loyalist statue and plaque in front of 50 Main Street East, Hamilton, Ontario by Saforrest (https://commons.wikimedia.org/wiki/File:United_Empire_Loyalist_statue_and_plaque_in_Hamilton,_Ontario.jpg)

Pg. 177
Lord Selkirk Statue by Arnaud Rossignon (https://commons.wikimedia.org/wiki/File:Lord-selkirk-statue.jpg)

Pg. 182
Unidentified Métis Woman by William James Topley. Topley Studio. Library and Archives Canada, e011156893 /William James Topley. Topley Studio. Bibliothèque et Archives Canada, e011156893. File edited. (https://commons.wikimedia.org/wiki/File:Unidentified_M%C3%A9tis_Woman_-_Femme_m%C3%A9tisse_non_identifi%C3%A9e_(24501008215).jpg)

Pg. 235
Lake in Dome Creek, British Columbia, Canada, April 2019 by Jakub Fryš (https://commons.wikimedia.org/wiki/File:Lake_in_Dome_Creek.jpg)

Pg. 240
Bay of Fundy at Low Tide by Eric Van Lochem (https://commons.wikimedia.org/wiki/File:Bay_of_Fundy_at_Low_Tide.jpg)

www.ingramcontent.com/pod-product-compliance
Lightning Source LLC
Chambersburg PA
CBHW030904080526
44589CB00010B/137